PASTORAL COUNSELING

BOOKS BY WAYNE E. OATES

Published by The Westminster Press

Pastoral Counseling

When Religion Gets Sick

On Becoming Children of God

Pastoral Counseling in Social Problems:
Extremism, Race, Sex, Divorce

The Christian Pastor
(REVISED AND ENLARGED EDITION)

Protestant Pastoral Counseling

The Revelation of God in Human Suffering

Anxiety in Christian Experience

The Bible in Pastoral Care

With Kirk H. Neely

Where to Go for Help
(REVISED AND ENLARGED EDITION)

PASTORAL COUNSELING

by WAYNE E. OATES

The Westminster Press
Philadelphia

PUBLISHED BY THE WESTMINSTER PRESS ®

PHILADELPHIA, PENNSYLVANIA

PRINTED IN THE UNITED STATES OF AMERICA

Library of Congress Cataloging in Publication Data

Oates, Wayne Edward, 1917–
  Pastoral counseling.

  1. Pastoral counseling. I. Title.
BV4012.2.O23   253.5   73–19719
ISBN 0–664–20992–0

Contents

Contents

Preface

The field of pastoral counseling as a professional discipline is gradually coming of age. The technical data being amassed in pastoral psychology is a body of information that is being used as a common base of reality for pastoral counselors. The processes and techniques of pastoral counseling have reached a remarkable degree of acceptance by pastors who have had an increasingly validated and standardized kind of clinical pastoral education. A great many books describe the methods of operation of the pastoral counselor, and these represent *tactical* manuals of great value.

I have sought to set forth in these pages a strategy and a Christian philosophy of pastoral counseling that have been deduced from the clinical practice of pastoral counseling, from dialogue with my colleagues in pastoral counseling from all over the country, and from the teaching and supervision of many highly competent students over the past twenty-five years. All of this experience has developed within the firm conviction and the tense ambiguities of perceiving my destiny as a Christian pastor—in the context of the fellowship of Christians and of the larger community of those who both care and are able to care wisely for other people.

The central focus of the book is upon the tensions brought by the ambiguities inherent in the identity and function of a pastor. The dilemmas involved in those ambiguities can be resolved only at the expense of accepting half-truths as a way of life rather than as fragile hypotheses for further correction of one's course in life.

I express my lasting gratitude to my fellow pastoral counselors Glenn Asquith, Ronald Bradley, Branson Dunn, Larry

Henderson, Wesley Monfalcone, and Kirk Neely. They were members of a clinical pastoral education group I supervised along with my colleagues Wade Rowatt and Daniel McKeever in the spring of 1973. Each section of this book has been thoroughly tested and explored by this group.

I am indebted, too, to Elaine Tutterrow, to her husband, Curtis, and to her little daughter, Cathy, for making her time and talents available to me for the typing of the manuscript and the search for innumerable references. She has been remarkably efficient and patient as she has worked at this task with high competence.

W. E. O.

Chapter 1

WHAT MAKES
COUNSELING PASTORAL?

Counseling, generally speaking, is a nonmedical discipline, the aims of which are to facilitate and quicken personality growth and development, to help persons to modify life patterns with which they have become increasingly unhappy, and to provide comradeship and wisdom for persons facing the inevitable losses and disappointments in life. The counselor's task is, as the French proverb puts it, *Guérir quelquefois, soulager souvent, consoler toujours,* i.e., to heal sometimes, to remedy often, to comfort always. Persons seeking counseling are usually suffering internal and interpersonal conflict. They feel the need to talk with a competent person who is not emotionally or socially involved in their lives. A counselor provides both objectivity and a reasonable degree of privacy for them, and they usually want to talk with a person who is trained and appropriately experienced. Therefore, counseling is ordinarily a formal relationship between a counselor and a counselee.

By "formal" I mean that counseling is conducted within specific time limits, and at a discreet and private place. Formal counseling involves an understanding in which the counselee consciously accepts the counselor *as* counselor. Neither counselor nor counselee confuses counseling relationships with other important relationships that human beings have such as those of friend, relative, lover, or professional colleague. Continued clarification is needed to keep confusion at a minimum. I have discussed this clarification extensively in *New Dimensions of Pastoral Care* (Fortress Press, 1970). Neither the counselor nor the counselee exploits the other for private emotional gratification. The communication between counselor and counselee, therefore, is therapeutic. The goals of healing are the reconciliation of conflicts through decision and the clarification of the purposes of life of the counselee through commitment. Furthermore, the communication in counseling is privileged: neither the counselor nor the counselee divulges his conversations to persons outside the relationship without the one first consulting the other.

The counseling relationship is focused upon the needs of the counselee. The central concern of the counselor is the quality of the relationship between the counselee and the counselor. The counseling process—however long or short in time—has a definite beginning, midphase, and ending. By its very nature, counseling is not the use of instant "word magic" to wave away the troubles of others. Neither is counseling the endless, lifelong supportive and emotionally nourishing process we find in a relative, a friend, or a colleague. However valuable these latter relationships may be in the everyday course of life, the counseling relationship becomes distorted if it is mistaken for these purposes.

Any preliminary definition of counseling in general tends to presuppose that the counselor has specialized training and experience. The counselor is assumed to have an institutional context for his work. As such, counseling is done by many professional persons today—guidance counselors, teachers, professors, personnel officers, military officers, lawyers, doctors, ministers, psychologists, social workers, etc. The question with which we are concerned here is: What is it that makes the work of the pastor as a counselor unique, that is, distinctly pastoral?

THE DISTINCTIVE CHARACTERISTICS
OF PASTORAL COUNSELING

One basic assumption of this book is that something makes counseling in general specifically pastoral. This is not to say that pastoral counseling is totally different from counseling in general, but it is to say that there is an area of expertise, a body of data, and a specific historical identity as a counselor which enables the pastor to bring a fresh consciousness and unique contribution to the general field of counseling. These specifics can be detailed as follows:

The God-in-Relation-to-Persons Consciousness in Counseling

Regardless of a counselor's professional identification, social role, and body of data in which he has expertise, that person's counseling becomes *pastoral* when the counselee or the counselor focuses the relationship upon the relation of God to the process of their lives. As Daniel Day Williams puts it, God becomes the third person in the relationship. Instead of being simply a dialogue, a *tri*alogue comes into being. Quite apart from the officialdom of therapeutic bureaucracies, *being* pastoral in one's counseling is not the private possession of paid, officially appointed priests. The reader can readily see that the point of view here is based upon the belief in the priesthood of all believers, including the counselee himself. Often, in spite of the protestations of the counselor or without his awareness of it, the counselee consciously reworks the counseling process into a God-in-relation-to-persons framework. When this happens, the counseling becomes pastoral.

On the other hand, just because an officially appointed, ecclesiastically ordained, and theologically educated pastor has the "office" of pastor, he is not exempt from the same disciplines required of counselors of other professional disciplines. The God-in-relation-to-persons frame of reference must necessarily be informed by the hard-earned factual data of other fields, such as philosophy, ethics, anthropology, psychology, medicine (especially psychiatry), and social work. Yet, for the pastor these become supporting data for the information which he uniquely brings to the counseling relationship. They become the basis for interprofessional collaboration rather than mere cooperation or amateurish competition.

This requirement came home clearly to me when I was collaborating with a private psychiatrist. Both he and I were seeing the same patient on different schedules with different objectives in mind, his psychiatric and mine pastoral. He said: "The patient is suffering from a great deal of perceptual distortion. My job as a physician is to clear up as much as I can the distortion, so that when the patient looks at God he can see God clearly. Your job is to see to it that when he looks at God he is looking at the right God and not the wrong one. That's what you are trained to do and I am not."

On another occasion a psychiatric resident asked me in a case conference, "What is it that you as a minister do in relation to a patient that I as a psychiatrist do not do?" I replied: "You have a choice as to whether you bring God into the focus of the patient's attention. I am different in that if I am introduced as a minister, I have no choice but that God tacitly or overtly becomes the focus of the relationship." The psychiatrist then asked, "Whose God becomes the focus of the relationship?" I replied, "The patient's God, not mine." The psychiatrist said: "Yes. That I know. But *who* is *your* God?" I replied that my God is the God and Father of our Lord Jesus Christ. Then she, the psychiatrist, said: "But I am a Hindu. How could you talk with me of God?" I replied that before she was a Hindu or I was a Christian we were both created by God as we later came to believe, but that as creatures, human beings, both of us are persons-in-relation-to-God as we know God. Therefore, we have much we can discuss if we are open to and teachable by each other. The entry of God into our discussion made the relationship pastoral whether we had entered into God-talk or not. The awareness was there.

God as Reality

The pastoral counselor's conception of what reality is differs from that of a nonpastoral counselor. The awareness of God *as* reality makes counseling pastoral. The conception of reality as mere conformity of the counselor or counselee to the least common denominator of social rectitude, conformity and acceptability, or even as the height of human wisdom in relation to the world is often what is meant by other counselors. Awareness of God is what Paul Tillich called the ultimate concern of persons. Overfixation upon proximate concerns is idolatry. The proximate concern of mental health, for example, can become an absolute value to the exclusion of everything else, and the distinctly human character of eccentricity and creativity will be missed. No one knows this better than one who has seen power-hungry staff members of a mental health center get into severe conflict with each other and begin trying to decide who is mentally sick among the staff itself. Such preoccupation is only a little less demonic than the quest of religious leaders for power through the use of varying norms of theological orthodoxy. The apostle Paul asked for a kind of militant humility when he described people who compared themselves with themselves and so proved themselves foolish. He asked for a "casting down of every high thing that exalts itself against the knowledge of God."

The prophetic concern for doing justly, loving mercy, and walking humbly with God is the "stance of being" and "angle of vision" that makes counseling pastoral. Much of other kinds of counseling consists of freeing people from the moralistic minutiae of cultural habits. Pastoral counseling does not neglect this. However, pastoral counseling is concerned with the growth of a mature conscience. The role and function of the professional minister as an ethicist *shape* the distinctly pastoral element in counseling, but they do not give it its charisma or substance. The basic data and unique tools of the pastor will not give him the sense of awe and wonder necessary to use them. Even the technical training in clinical settings now required for certification of pastoral counselors will not give the pastor the resolve and confidence to shift into a distinctly pastoral kind of counseling. To the contrary, the charisma and substance, the awe and wonder, the resolve and confidence necessary to relate to counselees as a uniquely pastoral counselor come from the counselor's own being-in-relation-to-God as an ethically serious thinker. Hence, the element of meditation, reflection, and communion with God about what is ethically serious—whether God is ever mentioned or not—pervades the pastoral counselor's personal perspective of life. To a large extent he has to shed his religious baby teeth. He can now sit still long enough to become a part of the agony of the souls of other people who are in moral confusion. He can absorb without too much fear the rebellion of the counselee against the idols others have named God. Pastoral counseling is sweaty participation with persons in their life-and-death struggle for moral integrity in relation to God. The pastoral counselor has "renounced the deeds that men hide for very shame; he neither practices cunning nor distorts the word of God; only by declaring the truth openly is he recommended [as counselor], and then it is to the common conscience of his fellowmen and in the sight of God." (Cf. II Cor. 4:2, NEB.)

Conversation About Faith in God

It would be easy for my reader to hear me pleading for a lot of God-chatter in the pastoral counseling relationship. It would be even easier for the reader who is in revolt against his own religious heritage and whose teeth have been set on edge against the sour religion eaten at a parent's table to understand me as some sort of God-talk exponent. However, let me say that this is not the case, even though I am unabashedly forthright in speaking of God in my own counseling when the occasion calls for it. At least three things need to be said here in order to clarify the issue of pastoral conversation about faith in and fellowship with God in the counseling situation.

First, I find common cause with Dietrich Bonhoeffer's word that we need to learn to speak of God in a secular manner. Pastoral counseling can be done without a counselor's being a phony holy Joe who sounds like Carl Sandburg's "contemporary bunkshooter." There are some inherently religious words, such as hope, joy, peace, care, love, concern, life, death, and verbs such as matter. When the scent of the counselor is programmed to sniff out the presence or absence of these in people's lives he begins to take on the characteristics of a *pastoral* counselor whether specifically religious jargon is ever used.

Second, the plain forthright discussion of God's relationship to this person has a heuristic value. Often the mention of God provokes and draws out hostility, feelings of injustice, despair, worthlessness, and alienation. The pastoral counselor may move to deep emotional levels of the person's life in a very brief span of time. More than that, *if* the pastor is indeed interested in *being* a pastor to the person, this clearly identifies his interest and concern. It gets the process going more rapidly. Edgar Draper, a psychiatrist, has gone even farther at this point. He says that using the religious ideation of a person as a way of seeing through life's difficulties often works when standard psychiatric and psychological media of communication do not yield results.

Yet pastors can easily be "cakes half turned," burnt on one side and half cooked on the other, in the use of language about and with God. Some pastors can *only* speak in a heavily programmed "holy speech." They are unaware of how they are being heard. Other pastors are so reticent or resistive to the use of any conversation about God or with God that a need of the counselee to converse at all about his relationship to God may be unattended, at best, and totally discounted as symptomatic of, "something else," at worst.

However, the pastoral counselor who sees things steady and

sees them whole can be more flexible. He sees the concern of people about their relationship to God as significant in its own right. A person's ultimate concern about life and death, hope and hopelessness, the feeling of being at home in the universe or being abandoned by all, and the need to be forgiven or left with a burden of sin because of real wrongdoing are real concerns, not just covers for something else. A pastor can sense the God-in-relation-to-persons nuances in seemingly profane or even vulgar and coarse expressions of these real concerns of his counselee. A good pastor is no fool, however. He knows when he is being manipulated by persons who want to change the subject from grimy ethical responsibilities to ethereal abstractions about moot religious arguments. He resists. In the name of God, he can get down to the real issues of divine truth and say to people who would argue about *where* to worship (as with the woman of Samaria): "Go get thy husband and bring him here," or some other appropriate but earthy word that needs to be said.

The Basic Data Bank of the Expertise of the Pastoral Counselor

Morris Taggart, of the Marriage and Family Consultation Center in Houston, in the American Association of Pastoral Counseling Information Project, asks the question: "Does there exist within the profession a 'body of knowledge,' a point of view, a way of understanding human events . . . which, although found among members of other professions, is somehow represented institutionally within this particular profession?" The specific body of data of the pastoral counselor is one of the factors that makes counseling in general *pastoral* in particular. As has been said, the pastoral counselor is not exempt from the disciplines required of other effective counselors. His work as a counselor depends upon the mastery of similar sources of knowledge about human personality as does theirs. In addition to this he has a body of data and insights of his own which he arrived at through intensive study, empirical research, and the laborious process of critical self-examination and the testing of hunches and hypotheses. In this the pastoral counselor is akin to and not exempt from demands upon the counselor of any other discipline. However, the distinctive body of data in which the pastoral counselor is expert can be identified as follows:

First, the pastoral counselor is an expert in the basic literature of his religion. The rabbi, the priest, and the minister in the Judeo-Christian traditions are experts in the Old and New Testaments, for example. The historical substratum, the guiding personalities, the stories, epics, poetry, parables, and the proverbs of these original sources are the area of his expertise. The pastoral counselor can identify cultural expressions of these teachings in the language, rituals, and behavioral compunctions of the counselee. For example, a distinguished psychologist, O. Hobart Mowrer, once said in a symposium that the Old Testament has much more to say about anxiety than does the New Testament. I challenged this on the grounds that Professor Mowrer had been reading the English Version of the New Testament, and probably the King James Version in English. In this sense, he was right. However, the Greek New Testament has a veritable pyrotechnic of insights about anxiety. I later wrote the book *Anxiety in Christian Experience* (The Westminster Press, 1955; reprinted by Word Books, 1971) and used the several meanings of anxiety in the New Testament as chapter heads and contents. When anxious people come to the pastoral counselor, he has in his knowledge of the Old and New Testaments an institutional representation of his expertise that is a part of his body of data.

In the second place, the pastoral counselor has detailed historical and contemporary data about the variegated forms of religious culture in the lives of the counselees with whom he counsels. He understands the Oriental and European backgrounds of these religious groups. Pastoral counselors have at their fingertips resource volumes that detail the teachings, rituals, and history of these groups. They know the Biblical basis of their beliefs; they know the ways in which these

Scriptural affirmations have been used, abused, and transmitted by particular religious groups. Pastoral counselors' training in church history is integral, therefore, to effective teamwork with other counselors. The other members of the healing team—psychologists, social workers, psychiatrists, etc. —expect him to *know* this. They ask about this.

For example, a middle-class black woman was admitted to a psychiatric unit. One of the positive factors of guidance and support in her life was the Bahai religion which she espoused. The pastoral counselor on the staff was asked at the therapeutic conference to prepare a one-page description of this religious group and its beliefs for use by the whole staff. A copy was placed by the resident psychiatrist in the chart of the patient. Thus it was recognized that while the psychiatric, psychological, and social work professions themselves have contributed much ancillary data to the pastoral counselor, they in turn have a remarkable void of knowledge about the general culture of their patients and particularly their patients' religious culture. This is due to specializations in their college educations, in many instances. Pastoral counselors, by means of their own specialization, have such data. The pastoral counselor should be an expert in the data of contemporary forms of religion. As an expert, he can contribute to other professionals. His expertise in this body of data is a hard core of what makes counseling pastoral and causes many counselees to come to him rather than to other counselors.

The Specific Community Resources of the Church

First and last, the pastoral counselor represents the church —for better or for worse—in the eyes of his counselee. This makes pastoral counseling uniquely pastoral. Many of the problems people present to a clergyman have religious overtones, even if they are not expressed. Whether or not the counselee is aware of the religious element inherent in his problem, the clergyman certainly recognizes it as such. Sometimes even a seemingly mundane problem can become attached to a larger question of the person's spiritual destiny under God and is set within the context of his religious community—past and/or present.

In the eyes of his counselee, the clergyman is the leader of the religious community. On the one hand, this gives him the privilege of taking the initiative toward people in times of need. On the other hand, it tends to prevent a clearly defined situation in which he is formally perceived as a counselor. The reason for this is that the clergyman must also function as preacher, teacher, administrator, and pastoral visitor in turn. In his own eyes, however, the clergyman sees himself always in the larger context of the pastor-parishioner relationship. As far as counseling goes, it means that he functions always as a pastoral counselor, not exclusively as a counselor. His work is distinguished always by the religious setting in which it is done. Both he and his counselee attach religious objectives, resources, and patterns of meaning to the counseling process. This is true whether or not the clergyman, depending upon the counselee and his problem, happens to choose religious terms to understand and to communicate with his counselee. The clergyman's counseling is incidental to, although inseparable from, his relationship to his total group.

In functioning as a counselor, therefore, the clergyman always does so as a representative leader of a religious community. This works out practically in several ways:

First, his responsibility to the total group limits the amount of time he can spend with any one individual, regardless of the amount of training he has as a counselor.

Second, his right to choose or select his counselees is limited.

Third, the clergyman is less free than other counselors to terminate his relationship to his counselees, inasmuch as he is enduringly related to them as communicant members of his congregation.

Fourth, the fact that a clergyman-counselor functions in the larger religious framework may be both a help and a hindrance to therapy. It would be a help to the extent that it would enable the counselee to relate readily in terms of confidence in the counselor. It would be a hindrance if the counselor were to use his position as a clergyman to dominate the counseling situation.

Finally, the pastor's leadership of a religious community puts him in touch with situations that would be considered "normal" by psychopathologists. Therefore his counseling must, as Howard Clinebell insists in his book *The People Dynamic* (Harper & Row, Publishers, Inc., 1972), develop both an individual and a group "therapy for normals." Consequently much pastoral counseling is of a preventive kind, such as premarital pastoral counseling, pastoral counseling of newlyweds, of the families of the dying, of persons facing surgery, of persons planning to change jobs or retire, of parents who have problems with their sons and daughters, and of persons with marriage conflicts.

The natural setting of the community of the church, *when scientifically perceived and utilized*, becomes an organism of relationships for providing miniature life-support systems for orphaned persons of all ages and conditions of life. The uniquely pastoral dimension of counseling rests in the distinctly communal character of the pastor's counseling. Not even *group* counseling, when done by a pastor, is done in isolation from the social fabric of the larger community.

The Prophetic Context of Pastoral Counseling

The fourth factor that makes pastoral counseling unique is the distinctly *public* character of the pastor's relationship, i.e., he speaks in public and is called upon to take public stands on controversial issues. He not only counsels with persons facing divorce or contemplating remarriage; he is answerable to a community on his position or point of view about divorce and remarriage. The pastoral counselor not only counsels the mother-to-be and/or father-to-be and/or grandparents-to-be about an unwanted pregnancy but is called upon to discuss the ethical issues about planned parenthood, birth control, and abortion at a public level as a teacher and preacher. The counselor not only confers with draft resisters in their acute isolation but must evaluate the matters of social justice involved in the ambiguities of amnesty for draft evaders in exile. When the pastoral counselor takes a stand, whatever it may be, he is publicly responsible and "takes the rap" of public opinion and controversy.

The pastoral counselor, therefore, is distinctive in that the illusion of ethical neutrality enjoyed by the purely private counselor is a luxury he cannot afford. The very nature of ordination as a minister rules out the luxury of a *purely* private ministry that ignores society as a whole. This ambiguity causes tension between the private and the public responsibilities of the pastoral counselor. The tension between being a private and a public person is the soil out of which pastoral counseling has grown. The reduction of this ambiguity and tension removes the distinctly prophetic element from the counseling. It may remain good counseling, in general, but it is no longer *pastoral* counseling, in particular, when this happens. Therefore, the central thrust of this book is upon the polarities of human suffering and the means of relieving them. The pastoral counselor has a prophetic responsibility to confer privately with individuals, groups, and populations. However, the counseling becomes pastoral when this privacy is not used as a sanctuary by the counselor. He speaks and writes to public audiences in behalf of the suffering people whom he serves privately. Consequently, he gets involved in social change and serves as an agent of social conscience about the broad-scale injustices in society. These injustices breed many of the problems of individuals and families, who come to the pastoral counselor. He cannot be detached from these, but must take a prophetic role in speaking for people who are helpless and oppressed, flayed and cast down like sheep without a shepherd. This makes counseling distinctly pastoral, also.

The Pastoral Counselor as an Ethicist

Another reality that makes counseling pastoral is when the counselor takes responsibility for dealing directly and frankly with ethical issues. The pastoral counselor's training, therefore, equips him with technical data and conceptual frames of reference. An example of technical data involving ethical decision and responsibility is the recent discovery of the technique of amniocentesis by gynecologists and other specialists in prenatal care of mothers and their babies. This method is a technique whereby an intrauterine fluid sample can be drawn during the first trimester of a pregnancy and tests made whereby exact predictions of some birth defects can be made. The couple is faced with the option of whether to allow the child to be born badly mentally deficient or to have a therapeutic abortion. Students in clinical pastoral education in Louisville, Kentucky, are regularly involved as *pastoral* counselors with these couples. They work alongside the psychologist, the social worker, and the physician. Their concrete assignment is to deal with the ethical issues involved.

Such pastoral counselors use the case method which consists of data collection, establishing a responsible and trustworthy relationship, and the clarification of the facts at an emotional level of acceptance rather than a purely rational computation of "the facts" to the couple. Students are faced as ethicists with either a choice or a combination of at least four conceptual approaches to the process of pastoral counseling of a couple facing such an ethical crisis. The first approach is a *forensic* one. The legal barriers and traditional biases in the couple's life must be a part of the data collection. For example, if one or both spouses is or are devout Catholics and consider any form of abortion to be against canonical law, they will have difficulty in carrying through with an abortion of this kind. If they consult only Catholic physicians, they are faced with the availability of ethical medical care. The second conceptual approach to the ethical crisis of therapeutic abortion is a *contextual* one in which the total milieu of the people involved and their investments, rights, and needs will be considered, weighed, and empathically understood in search of mercy, justice, and humility before God. The third possible conceptual frame of reference is a *situational* approach in which the dictates of love of God and neighbor are evaluated *de novo* without regard to tradition, law, or even the total context of other peripherally related people in the milieu. The fourth such frame of reference possible is a *covenantal* approach in which the kind of prior agreements, understandings, and commitments the couple have made to each other, to their other children, to other important persons, and to God are carefully assessed. For example, to commit oneself consciously to the care of a seriously retarded child involves one's commitments to one's spouse to have or not have children. If there are other children, their conception and birth was a commitment to their well-being. Does this fresh commitment contravene already established covenants? New covenants are not easily or wisely formed at the total expense of prior covenants.

Therefore, with basic technical data and a conscious use of known frames of concept in ethics, the pastoral counselor ponders with the counselee "the shape of things to come," the forms of justice and love in the here and now, and the weight of the past in the process of ethical decision and responsible ethical living.

The Power to Bless or Withhold Blessing

Withal, the ethical struggle just described is a sterile and academic process if the *pastoral* counselor does not realize that the couple look to a pastoral counselor in a unique way: they look upon him in their struggles as one who blesses or withholds a blessing. They want to know and to feel that he knows and feels that they are "all right" with God. This is what Paul Pruyser and Myron Madden call the pastoral blessing. Madden says that the power to bless is the starting of genuine self-acceptance at a point outside the self: "It must come from another self who has been able in turn to accept healing from his own brokenness. The other and outside person cannot intrude or force himself into the picture. He must be authorized or given the power by the broken one to accept and heal. . . . Just as one life comes from another life, so blessing comes from another." (Myron C. Madden, *The Power to Bless*, pp. 141–142; Abingdon Press, 1970.) Paul Pruyser says that this power to bless demarcates pastors' "office and functions from those of other caretakers, healers, guides, and teachers." For the pastors to relinquish or fear to use this power and refuse to think of the role of blessing in counseling is "a dear price to pay for one's own secularization!" (Paul Pruyser, "The Master's Hand: Psychological Notes on Pastoral Blessing," William B. Oglesby, Jr., ed., *The New Shape of Pastoral Theology*, pp. 364–365; Abingdon Press, 1969.)

Yet the exercise of this authority is the source of its power. It takes courage and initiative on the part of the pastor. The authenticity and truthfulness of the power lies in the communion of the pastor with God. The practice of the pastoral blessing seems to move through a threefold process: (1) *Confession*. This is the discipline of listening to the grim and often tawdry details of the person's confession of despair, loneliness, rebellion, exploitation of others, and shame over not having even achieved the minimum of his aspirations in life. This takes time, energy, careful questioning, and a disciplined childlike openness to sit still and quiet long enough to let the person "pour out his complaint before the Lord," as did Hannah with Eli. (2) *Decision-making and behavior modification*. In classical religious literature this is often called penance or restitution. It is the demonstration of new behaviors that are reinforced positively and blessed with the encouragement of the pastoral counselor. (3) *Forgiveness*. This is the communication of the good news that God has forgiven the person, accepts him, and wants his fellowship and companionship. This is the forthright attempt to remove the "curse character" of the past and to affirm, bless, and consecrate the present and the future. This is the core of the power to bless—forgiveness that enables the person to forgive those who have transgressed against him. The blessed then begin to become a blessing.

This process of blessing is uniquely theological in that it takes place in the context of the God-in-relation-to-persons awareness, it is overseen by a person—a "parson"—skilled in the word of the Scripture, the knowledge of religious history, the technical data and conceptual frames of reference of an ethicist, and brought alive by his daring to bring the blessing of God to the person in need. These are some of the things that make counseling pastoral.

Chapter 2

A POINT OF VIEW

Scientific approaches to pastoral counseling have been used since Rollo May's book *The Art of Counseling* appeared in 1939. Later, Seward Hiltner pioneered with his definitive book, *Pastoral Counseling.* Since then extensive literature has appeared that deals with the "how to" of pastoral counseling in specific settings such as the hospital, the church, and the clinic. Other books have set pastoral counseling in the context of specific problem areas of life such as marriage, death and dying, the mentally ill, alcoholism and drug abuse, unwed mothers, and in relation to the content and substance of the Christian faith. This substantial and reliable body of literature is in large part highly dependable and does not need reduplication. But one of the weaknesses of much of the literature just mentioned is that we as authors tend to begin *de novo,* as if no one else had ever written on the subject. As a result we may justly be accused of being repetitious. Pastoral counseling as a field has suffered from a lack of conceptual orientation of its own. The need, therefore, it seems to me, is for a book that is devoted to the development of a balanced conceptual orientation. I assume the validity of techniques and know-how in already existing manuals of pastoral counseling procedure, casebooks, etc. A list of these appears at the end of this chapter.

Consequently, I would like to state a comprehensive point of view that may become a part of the conceptual overview of the reader as he does the work of pastoral counseling. That point of view or hypothesis is simply stated: Pastoral counseling is unique in that pastoral wisdom, developed through the history of synagogue, temple, and church, refuses to permit the therapeutic enthusiasms of the moment to enchant the pastor with one side or another of the great polarities that characterize human nature. If he takes the pastoral heritage seriously, it will not permit him to become overidentified with recurrent "corrective" therapies that have emerged from time to time. Corrective therapies are reactions against some former therapy which in itself neglected vital realities in human experience and behavior. Pastoral counseling, to the contrary, is characterized by the affirmation of the tension that exists between the seemingly contradictory demands laid upon the counselor. The pastoral counselor insists upon the *whole* counsel of God as over against half-truths. A particular one-sided emphasis may provide comfort and even luxury for counselors. Yet to settle for one side of an ambiguous human necessity requires that one be willing to settle for a kind of therapy that negates and removes these tensions. By insisting on acceptance of the ambiguity of human suffering the pastoral counselor can make a separate contribution of his own to the generalities of therapy.

PARADOXES OF PASTORAL COUNSELING

My hypothesis can be made clearer by identifying the paradoxical tensions which the pastoral counselor affirms, accepts, and lives with in his counseling. These several ambiguities of pastoral counseling will be the substance and outline of the rest of this book. Therefore, it is important that they be identified in brief detail here. Doing so will tend both to clarify the hypothesis of the book and to map out the pattern of discussion. I have chosen to identify eight paradoxes or ambiguities of pastoral counseling.

1. The Institutional and the Personal

The pastor, by the very nature of the pastoral office, is committed in advance to the tension between the institutional necessities of the church *and* to caring for individuals whose participation in the institutional life of the church is not possible at many levels. The church as an institution has its doctrinal basis, its economic support, its social and ethical involvement or lack of involvement, and a history of the particular group of churches to which it belongs. Yet, unless that church is like salt that has lost its savor, it also has the call to care for the individual, personal needs of people whether they are part of the church or not. For example, in dealing with individuals and families, a pastoral counselor is often caught between the demand of his congregation to recruit new members and the quiet personal desperation of the individuals and families which precludes his making recruitment for the church a primary concern. This tension and ambiguity is inescapable. The pastoral counselor cannot lightly settle the strain on one side or the other. He is committed to *both* the institutional *and* the personal dimension of life.

2. Theological Continuity and Scientific Discontinuity

The disciplined and clinically trained pastor is obligated to maintain the *continuities* that the theological realities of life represent. At the same time the pastoral counselor has to stay abreast of the ever-changing and developing *discontinuities* of the psychological and social sciences. He cannot function as a sort of Melchizedek who has no heritage, but must plumb this heritage for its relevance to the less poetic and historically sensitive psychosocial sciences. Psychotherapies come and go. The pastor must keep each passing emphasis in touch with what David Roberts rightly called "a

Christian view of man." The changing emphases in pastoral
counseling seem to suggest great discontinuity unless the
pastor has a full-orbed view of the backdrop of Christian
understandings of man as a basis for continuity. The primacy
and continuity of his heritage keeps the pastor from mere
eclecticism. He does not just pick and choose this and that
from various scientific therapies. Rather, he exercises critical
appraisal of their strengths and limitations from his historical,
theological, and ethical knowledge.

3. Training and Charisma

The pastoral counselor bears in his person the ambiguity
between professional know-how and training, on the one
hand, and the sense of being "given" the ministry, being
committed and set apart as a representative of God, on the
other hand. The pastoral counselor sees the ministry of counseling as both achievement and gift, personal discipline and
spontaneous response to the Spirit of God. The effective pastor
will not let either the piety or the pride of other pastors or
the technical competence of other professionals push him into
the corner of a purely serendipitous dependence upon some
vague spirit *or* a method-actor dependence upon some tried
and tested technique of counseling. Pastoral counseling is
both professional and charismatic, both traditional and neotraditional, and both scientific and mystical.

4. Durable vs. Short-Term Relationships

In both pastoral counseling and other kinds of counseling
and psychotherapy, the issue is regularly raised: How long
shall therapy last? Psychoanalysis has classically held out for
a longer-term, more-frequent-interview kind of therapy. Revi-
sionists have sought to develop short-term forms of psychotherapy. The pastor is in an ambiguous position because of the
multiple nature of pastoral relationships. The pastoral counselor may at one and the same time be the neighbor, the
pastor-preacher, and the counselor of a given person. The
pastoral counselor cannot easily decide that he is going to

have a precisely timed, limited-to-a-certain-number-of-interviews counseling relationship. The durability of the longer pastoral relationship is set over against the temporariness of a certain dimension of the dialogue known as counseling. This paradox will need careful exploration. Durable relationships are necessary contexts for specialized relationships of pastoral counseling. Yet every relationship has some sort of end. The *eschaton* with its anxiety of finitude pervades pastoral counseling.

5. *Aggressive and Passive Pastoral Counseling*

The pastoral counselor is called upon to be both aggressive and passive in the effort to care for people. The prerogative of his function as pastor provides both the opportunity and the necessity for taking initiative at times. On the other hand, the more passive waiting stance is equally indigenous to the work of the pastoral counselor. Yet he cannot say: "I cannot help someone until he asks for it." Nor can the pastoral counselor be so aggressive as to be the one who always takes the initiative. Rather, initiative must be calibrated with varying degrees of aggressiveness. A varied set of tools for gaining entrée into people's confidence is available to the pastor. One's use of these tools of initiative uniquely expresses the identity of the pastor as a counselor.

6. *Private and Public Ministries*

The pastoral counselor works both privately and publicly with counselees in ways not characteristic of many counselors. Reference to this has already been made in the first chapter. However, the skillful management of the public-private continuum calls for detailed attention in this conceptualization of the work of the pastoral counselor. The private-public ambiguity involves the handling of information, such as public knowledge, privileged communication, and confessional data. The responsibility of the pastor to deal with the social dimen-

sion of individual, private problems also is involved in this paradox.

7. *The Individual and the Group*

There was a time when pastoral counseling was seen as a
purely individual, one-to-one relationship. Little was done by
pastors that would be called group counseling. Now the pen-
dulum has swung to the other extreme. One hears pastoral
counselors of considerable renown saying that to work with
individuals is a waste of time. The group is the thing. However, the point of view here is that both of these are half-
truths. The settlement of the issue on one side of the ambiguous needs of individuals and groups is to miss the thing that
makes counseling distinctly pastoral. The hard reality is that
pastors cannot choose to work with individuals or groups;
they work with both, and the hallmark of their skill is in
balancing the two in relation to each other in a responsible
and skilled manner. Detailed attention to the interaction of
individual and group pastoral counseling will provide data
for an extensive study of the process of pastoral counseling.

The relationship of the individual to the group extends to
the pastor's work as both a reconciler of social conflicts and
a catalyst of conflict for the common good. A tension is drawn
between his role as a mediator and reconciler on the one hand
and that of a challenger and confronter on the other hand.
Does the pastor take sides in controversial issues, or remain
neutral and seek to mediate? Until recent developments in
social action and the politics of confrontation, it was simply
assumed that the work of the minister was always that of the
reconciler who sought to improve communication, develop
effective compromises, and be a peacemaker. However, this
may do away with the prophetic task such as that described
by Jesus when he said that he came not to bring peace but
a division. The agony of being *pastoral* counselors is that
both horns of this dilemma are theirs to handle. To forfeit

one or the other is to miss the dimension of suffering in the work of the pastoral counselor.

8. *Family Ties and Liberation*

The final ambiguity which continually attends the pastor as a counselor is his combined responsibility to nurture and sustain close-knit nuclear family ties and at the same time be a part of liberating persons from overdependence upon parents so that they can fulfill the gospel by becoming a part of the larger family of mankind. Recent ethical and social challenges of the conventional family structure through "trial living together," communal family living, and even group sex are secular demands for a distinctly religious and ethical answer to the relation of the nuclear family to its larger community. Women's liberation is causing us to ask searching questions about unreflective stereotypes of women and especially of those who are mothers. The condition and need of single persons, widows and widowers, and divorced persons are such as can no longer go unheeded by the pastor and the church. Yet, the need for continuity of commitment makes the bonds of the nuclear family equally as important to him as a pastor and to the fellowship of the church as an extended family.

At the points of these eight ambiguous paradoxes, the pastoral counselor has a wisdom to offer other professional counselors that will contribute to the upgrading of their function. The pastoral counselor has too long stood as supplicant before the behavorial scientists. He has not dared to challenge them as they have settled for narrowed certainties on one side or the other of the paradoxes. Humility in relationship to the behavioral scientists can no longer be a nice name for obsequiousness. Authentic humility is a by-product of a confidence of the pastoral counselor as to what a balanced human wisdom in counseling of any kind truly is.

The question arises: How can a minister absorb, survive, and transcend the suffering that the tension between these ambiguities entails? First, I would suggest that much of the suffering is resolved when the minister decides that the ambiguities are normal, ceases to fret about the fact that they do not go away, and accepts them as inherent in being a minister. Secondly, the minister can enjoy the broader base of wisdom that accepting the ambiguities affords him. He does not suffer nearly as much as when he knows or suspects that he is half-baked, half-cocked, *and* halfhearted! Thirdly, the minister can maintain his balance under the tension by taking the initiative to share his feelings of ambiguity and wistfulness for simplicity with a collegium or group of fellow ministers. Finally, as Paul Tillich says in the last volume of his *Systematic Theology* (The University of Chicago Press, 1963), the life of the Spirit involves the transcendence of ambiguity of human existence through faith in and prayer to God.

BOOKS ON COUNSELING

Berne, Eric, *Transactional Analysis in Psychotherapy.* Grove Press, Inc., 1961.

Bonnell, John Sutherland, *Pastoral Psychiatry.* Harper & Brothers, 1938.

Bradford, Leland P., Gibb, Jack R., and Benne, Kenneth (eds.), *T-Group Theory and Laboratory Method.* John Wiley & Sons, Inc., 1964.

Buber, Martin, *I and Thou,* 2d ed. Charles Scribner's Sons, 1958.

Cabot, Richard, and Dicks, Russell, *The Art of Ministering to the Sick.* The Macmillan Company, 1936.

Clinebell, Howard, *Basic Types of Pastoral Counseling.* Abingdon Press, 1966.

Dinkmeyer, Don C., and Muro, James J., *Group Counseling: Theory and Practice.* F. E. Peacock Publishers, Inc., 1971.

Frankl, Viktor, *Man's Search for Meaning.* Pocket Books, Inc., 1963.

Freud, Sigmund, *A General Introduction to Psychoanalysis.* Pocket Books, Inc.

Glasser, William, *Reality Therapy.* Harper & Row, Publishers, Inc., 1965.

Golembiewski, Robert T., and Blumberg, Arthur (eds.), *Sensitiv-*

ity Training and the Laboratory Approach. F. E. Peacock Publishers, Inc., 1970.

Hiltner, Seward, *The Counselor in Counseling*. Abingdon Press.

———— *Pastoral Counseling*. Abingdon-Cokesbury Press, 1952.

———— *Theological Dynamics*. Abingdon Press, 1972.

———— and Colston, Lowell, *The Context of Counseling*. Abingdon Press, 1961.

Knowles, Joseph, *Group Counseling*. Prentice-Hall, Inc., 1964.

Lieberman, Morton A., Yalom, Irvin D., and Miles, Matthew B., *Encounter Groups: First Facts*. Basic Books, Inc., 1973.

Madden, Myron C., *The Power to Bless*. Abingdon Press, 1970.

May, Rollo, *The Art of Counseling*. Abingdon-Cokesbury Press, 1939.

Oates, Wayne, *The Christian Pastor*, rev. ed. The Westminster Press, 1964.

———— *Protestant Pastoral Counseling*. The Westminster Press, 1962.

———— (ed.), *An Introduction to Pastoral Counseling*. The Broadman Press, 1959.

Oglesby, William B., Jr. (ed.), *The New Shape of Pastoral Theology*. Abingdon Press, 1969.

Perls, Frederick, Hefferline, Ralph, and Goodman, Paul, *et al.*, *Gestalt Therapy*. The Julian Press, Inc., 1951.

Roberts, David, *Psychotherapy and a Christian View of Man*. Charles Scribner's Sons, 1950.

Rogers, Carl, *Client-centered Therapy*. Houghton Mifflin Company, 1951.

Satir, Virginia, *Conjoint Family Therapy*, rev. ed. Science and Behavior Books, Inc., 1968.

Schaefer, Halmuth, and Martin, Patrick, *Behavioral Therapy*. McGraw-Hill Book Co., Inc., 1969.

Sullivan, Harry Stack, *The Psychiatric Interview*. W. W. Norton & Company, Inc., 1955.

Tillich, Paul, *The Courage to Be*. Yale University Press, 1952.

Treatment of Families in Conflict, formulated by The Committee on the Family, Group for the Advancement of Psychiatry. Science House, 1970.

Warner, W. Lloyd, *Social Class in America*. Yale University Press, 1960.

Wise, Carroll, *Pastoral Counseling: Its Theory and Practice*. Harper & Brothers, 1951.

Chapter 3

THE INSTITUTIONAL
AND THE PERSONAL

The pastoral counselor usually walks the narrow ridge between the demands of the institutions that support him and the needs of the personal lives of the people with whom he counsels. Often the needs of these persons coincide with the needs of the institutions. Then the pastoral counselor has respite from the tension between these needs. More often they conflict. Then the pastoral counselor bears the weight of the demands of the church as an institution conflicting with his commitment to care for the deeply personal needs of individuals, families, and small groups. This chapter is a careful study of this twin demand upon the pastoral counselor and the suggestion of some ways to manage this demand.

SOME PURPOSES OF THE WORKING CHURCH

I refer to the "working church" rather than to a nebulous church-in-general. I affirm the meaning of the Kingdom of God as the fellowship of those—gathered or scattered—who are known to each other in the increase of love of God and neighbor. H. Richard Niebuhr gave rich meaning to the purpose of the church and its ministry in his book, *The Purpose of the Church and Its Ministry* (pp. 27–38; Harper & Brothers, 1956).

The church and its ministry survives on the purpose of the increase of the love of God and neighbor.

Some additional purposes of the individual church emerge, however, when one begins to counsel with individuals and families in the context of the particular church of which he is pastor. American churches are voluntary organizations. They are supported by freewill offerings of individuals and families. They are not supported by taxation of the general population, by foundation (ordinarily), nor by any such steady sources of supply. The minister is the person in charge of raising his own salary. The minister more often than not is given a vote of confidence or of no confidence by the way the members of the church give money. The giving pattern of the members is closely related to their attendance pattern. The economics of financial support and church attendance add to the minister's purpose as one who is committed along with his congregation to the increase of the love of God and neighbor and several subpurposes that shape his function as a pastoral counselor.

A Place of Meeting

The increase of love of God and neighbor happens *somewhere*. Pastoral counseling is a meeting that happens in a place. Existentially, such a meeting of love of God and neighbor can happen anywhere. The meeting can happen in the marketplace, where people bump into each other serendipitously. The increase of the love of God and neighbor through pastoral counseling can happen in places of business, schools, and industries. The earliest places of worship and counsel seem to have been in homes. As new religious groups are formed today, they tend to meet in homes. Then buildings are rented or borrowed. Then lands are bought and buildings are planned. The construction of a church building symbolizes what the congregation perceives to be its purpose. (Does it take into account the needs of persons for counseling?) In any event, the acts of building a church structure can become an overriding demand upon the attention of the pastor and the congregation. Buying real estate and paying for buildings take time, money, and energy. The pastor's attention is soaked up along with his time and energy. Considerable time is spent in arbitrating disputes among the congregation as to how much building is needed, how the floor space should be allotted, and how it should be decorated.

The pastor's relationship to individuals and families who have personal needs for counseling is affected directly and indirectly by the "real estate" demands for his attention. Real estate can absorb his attention completely to the neglect of both his preaching and his counseling. As a friend, I was visiting in the hospital with a man suffering from an early arteriosclerosis. Our conversation revolved around his preoccupation with an impending divorce from his wife, his fear of being left alone as a sick man, and his feeling that he had sinned against God. His pastor came into the room during the visit. The subjects of the pastor's conversation were that this man had been doing a "fine job as chairman of the building committee," that offerings the day before had been good, and that the man should be congratulated. Later this man and his wife came to me for private personal counseling. They told me that their pastor did not know anything of the situation. They felt that he was too burdened with the planning of the new church building to bother him.

However, in counseling with them myself, I was faced with an even more subtle pressure than the pastor. At that time, a certain chaplaincy program in which I was deeply interested was woefully unsupported financially. This couple had no claim on my time except as friends. Yet they were an affluent couple. To what extent was I to use my relationship to them to "raise money" for the chaplaincy?

Let us hypothetically thicken the plot by asking this question. Let us suppose that this couple *did* confide their problem and concern in the pastor who was in the midst of the building program. To what extent would the pastor himself feel his building program jeopardized by the impending marital breakup of his building committee chairman? To what extent, on the other hand, would he be tempted, as I was, to use the counselees as "means" for financing the program of the building? Would their giving be a side effect of being really helped, or would it be the focus of the attention of the pastor?

This situation demonstrates my hypothesis. The pastor cannot disavow either the responsibility of providing a place of meeting for his congregation or his responsibility to give them guidance about an intense problem such as an impending divorce. He can get additional persons to help him do both these things well. He cannot, however, let his attention be so completely absorbed by either that the other is ignored, selectively inattended, or denied as a responsibility.

Some pastors think that leaving the pastoral ministry for the chaplaincy or teaching will solve this dilemma. What a fantasy! At this very time, I am both working at the task of finding adequate floor space for a counseling service in our school setting and counseling with individuals who need attention about problems such as premarital planning, deep and private confessional situations, and regular week-by-week counseling sessions with individuals and groups. Similar problems of support and supply, on the one hand, and actual combat with the personal and group needs of persons, on the other hand, appear in the chaplaincy and the teaching ministry. Even if one decides that he is going to do full-time counseling in the setting of a counseling center, the logistics of providing a place to meet counselees and groups still must be carried out simultaneously.

The crucial factor in dealing with the logistics of providing a practical place for counseling rests in the way in which physical plant and building priorities become the be-all and end-all of the ministry of a pastor. When one is working with different social classes of persons, the place where one meets may become an impediment to ministry on three counts. First, it may be so squalid and shabby that people of the upper classes will not frequent it. Second, it may be so plush and affluent that even people of considerable means will resent having to pay freewill offerings or fees for such opulence. People of the blue-collar classes will avoid such a setting.

Somewhere between these two unwise extremes rests the decision. Third, the place may symbolize a kind of counseling a counselee does not want. He may not want to be seen in a church because of painful memories or stereotypes of churches. He may not want to be seen at a psychiatric clinic because of other adverse memories or stereotypes, etc.

In any place, the pastoral counselor must have a "shepherding" perspective rather than a "temple" perspective of his work as counselor. The shepherd uses a place in terms of its nourishing function for those for whom he cares. The temple-oriented minister uses a place in terms of the status, prestige, and official sanction it provides for him.

Missionary Outreach and Membership Growth

A second purpose of most churches is to have their membership grow in size. This purpose is inextricably intertwined with the missionary outreach of the church. Pastors who are genuinely interested in getting to the deeper levels of people's suffering often find that their motives are suspect. The person may assume that their sole purpose is to "get joiners" in their particular church. Pastoral visitation often goes threadbare because no other purpose than recruitment of new members is considered by the pastor. I recall a poignant example of a pastor who had settled his ministry so completely on the side of missionary outreach and the recruitment of members to the point that he said: "I have so many people coming to see me about their fears of committing suicide, about marriage problems, and about their troubles with their children that I never have any time to spread the gospel!" On the other hand, I have seen pastors who were so concerned with the kinds of problems this pastor mentioned that they did not see themselves as communicators of the good news of God in Jesus Christ. The easy way to do ministry is to *resolve* the ambiguity between caring for persons and building an institution in these ways. The tension between the two identifies the distinctly pastoral counselor in the working church.

The tension between missionary outreach and direct care

for the beings of persons is not a new problem. It is so old that many no longer feel it, much less deal with it creatively.

European influences of the hope for a "religious establishment" that would *as an institution* control both the political and the economic life of America came to America before the American Revolution. The dreams of power and influence formed the militant Protestantism of New England and Southern colonies. The ministry was supported, for example, by law in the Ministry Act of 1693 in four of the ten colonies. "Anglican establishments were provided for in Maryland (1702), North and South Carolina (1706, 1715), and finally in Georgia (1758)." (Robert T. Handy, *A Christian America: Protestant Hopes and Historical Realities,* p. 11; Oxford University Press, Inc., 1971.) The "establishment" of religion was socially shattered by the American Revolution and independence and legally forbidden in the Constitution. However, the missionary zeal of religious groups maintained the dream of identifying their particular form of Protestantism with political and economic control of the whole culture. Many Protestants still hold to this illusion. Their forms and congregations of piety are enclaves of the past in a post-Protestant era. As Handy says, "If some Protestants continue to think and work as though the virtual identification of their religion and American civilization is still viable, or that with a little more effort America will become a Christian nation in their terms, they will be seriously hampered in playing a creative role for human good that a religious movement can exercise in a modern cultural situation." (*Ibid.,* p. 214.)

The cultural imperialism of individual churches, aided and abetted by the denominations of which they are usually a part, is a subtle and self-deceiving part of "public image conscious" pietism. The minister easily is lured and lures himself into seeing recruitment of members, common agreement upon standards of behavior, and the success of his organization as the service which those to whom he ministers owe the church. *Their* needs are secondary. Yet those early findings of research indicate that the church's loss of members is correlated with their feeling that the church abandoned them after the first glow of its success in recruiting them. Especially did they feel abandoned in the mid and later stages of grief, in the aftermath of separation and/or divorce, in the long vigil of anxiety about sons in the draft and in war, and in retirement. In seeking to resolve the ambiguity between building church membership and meeting people's deeper needs by overfocusing on the former, the membership itself was lost.

On the other side of the ambiguity, no matter how well personal counseling and care needs are met, the life of a community begins to stagnate and inbreed if no new lives are incorporated. The abdication of any outreach can be devastating also. The ambiguity itself must be affirmed, accepted, and borne. Yet people must be counseled for their own sakes and not as means of any kind.

My own sense of this ambiguity has always been that an effective perception of and ministry to the deepest hurts of people produces side effects of recruitment that are more salutary than massive programs of outreach. For example, a young minister of music recently was greatly concerned that one of his choir members had withdrawn from the choir. She ceased to come to church. His attempts to persuade her to return had failed. He took time with her in an office visit one day to converse about her feelings on the subject of retirement. He invited her to come for another interview. She later returned to the choir with no persuasion from him.

Cultural Respectability

Attendance upon church activities is one of the signs in our society that a person is moving into cultural respectability. The person who unites with a church has decided to have done with the things that are unrespectable. He aims to present to the world a solid witness of a clean and proper life, free of any of the things that the particular group identifies as unacceptable. Forms of behavior, customs of dress, manners of speech, become very important. Such a concern for respecta-

bility is a struggle to be somebody after having felt like a
nobody.

Coupled with this surge toward cultural respectability is a
certain kind of social camaraderie that varies from church to
church. Pure loneliness pushes many people to church. They
seek "fellowship," being welcome, etc. Yet this camaraderie
can be somewhat stylized and routine, superficial and repres-
sive. Church dinners, socials, coffees, teas, and the like may
become occasions for much standing around, engaging in light
tête-à-tête, shaking hands with people, having short greetings
with everyone, and smiling considerably. This is true even of
the revival meeting. Churches of the tradition of the Great
Awakening today accompany revival meetings with a heavy
round of entertainment, eating, and engaging in much festivity.
Revivals grew to a peak of enthusiasm in rural America when
social gatherings were few, centered largely in church or at a
barroom, and loneliness was assuaged by both in different
ways. These revivals were usually after cotton crops were
"laid by" and cotton-picking time was yet to be. On ranches,
the completion of roundup time was also a time of celebration. Festivity was the order of the day. Revivals fitted these
schedules in timing. Consequently, the tradition of social festivity both competed with the revival in objectives and co-
operated with it in time and drawing a crowd. Entertainment
was needed. Both the revival and the barroom provided a
different and competing kind. In the church, the motif of
festivity prevailed.

One must appreciate the need for play, festivity, and celebration in the fellowship of faith. Room should be made for
such activities. However, they can simmer away to meaningless rituals of superficial eating and smiling routines. Nothing
can be more deadening to depth conversation or to high
celebration. One cannot be cynically averse to fellowship with
people, to smiling occasionally, or to shaking hands with
friends. Yet these occasions and the cultural respectability
they represent *can* insulate the minister and the church from
the more profound needs of the membership itself, to say

nothing of those who are not a part of the respectable circle. The coffee-and-cake routine can clip the slender thread of communication with persons in times of despair over life-and-death issues.

One might call this coffee-and-cake routine the Martha-and-Mary routine, also. "Martha was distracted with much serving." Mary "sat at the Lord's feet and listened to his teaching." The preoccupation of a pastor and his congregation with relatively superficial "activities" may short-circuit any serious conversation about their spiritual heritage, the decisive issues of life they are facing, or the outcome of their lives. Fidelity to the church is measured by frequency of attendance upon all the meetings of the church, participation on committees of the church, and doing the chores of the church. Equal numbers of hours in profound conversation with members of the church are intangible, invisible, but do not count in measuring fidelity to the institution of the church.

All three of these *cultural* necessities of the institutional church—respectability needs, social club needs, and busywork needs—tend to produce a *denial* of personal or family conflict, stress, or disaster. People in the church tend to deny that either they or their fellow church members have any such distress. They refuse to provide funds for specialized assistance of themselves and their fellow communicants. They refuse to create innovations in the church program to provide for meeting these deeper chaotic distresses of their congregation.

Such generalizations as given in the last paragraph tend to be more true of lower-middle-class, upper-middle-class, and lower-upper-class congregations than of others. However, these classes provide the bulk of the "active" (in the sense used above) membership of the churches of America.

A case in point illustrates, if it does not verify, my contention. A layman and a laywoman in an upper-middle-class church saw the need for a young skilled social worker to be a member of the church staff to help counsel with the adolescent group in the church. They particularly wanted a psychiatric social worker. They offered to pay the salary of this person without her income having to be "billed" to the church budget. They were glad for her to be called as "youth counselor."

When the pastor presented this to the official board, it was refused by a majority vote, although a small minority were in favor of it. The reason given was that "we do not have any emotionally disturbed persons among our young people." At that time four of the adolescents were in private psychiatric hospitals in the city. Physicians were treating them; other ordained ministers were collaboratively working with physicians, pastor, and family.

I am not at all certain but that the latter health delivery system is not the more theologically viable approach for a church to take than to employ one person to whom to delegate the care needed. This assumes a pastor who is secure and astute enough to mobilize the professional skills of persons in the church. This solution is fine, in that instance, but it leaves two huge, unsolved problems in the case cited: first, the official denial of human suffering by an official board; and, second, any clear way of recognizing that time given by skilled persons is at least as tangible a service to the church as an institution as attending the business meetings of the church! Yet the purpose of the church in maintaining the denial mechanisms for respectability's sake leaves no room for dealing with the crucial needs of individuals or for bearing public witness to the purpose of the church to increase the love of God and neighbor where it hurts most *within* the church.

In fact, these unresolved problems can be cited as causes —though not the only ones—for the growth of pastoral counseling as a specialty of the ministry. Several alternative solutions of the denial-respectability purpose of the church as an obstacle to ministry have been and are being used.

Breaking the Barriers of Denial and Respectability

Several solutions, accommodations, or circumventions of the barriers of denial and respectability needs in the institutional church have emerged both in the past and in the present scenes. Any one of these or a combination of them can be found in attempts to break through the barriers of denial and the maintenance of respectability. Pastoral counseling as an art has been both encouraged and frustrated in its growth by the barriers of denial and respectability. Pastoral counseling as a private, confidential relationship to persons quite invisible to the rest of the congregation is a necessity if the parishioner is to get any help from his pastor on issues that defy the mores of respectability. Middle-class people seem to require this at the private, personal level. One could ask as I did in 1966 in my book *Pastoral Counseling in Social Problems* (p. 77; The Westminster Press, 1966): "Is pastoral counseling as we know it a prim, middle-class phenomenon?" The same thing could be asked about psychotherapy as practiced by other professions—psychology, psychiatry, and psychoanalysis. The middle-class person's need for privacy and his ability to pay for it encourage the growth of pastoral counseling and psychotherapy.

The same forces of denial and respectability, however, frustrate the growth of pastoral counseling in two ways: first, the middle-class person is not likely—at the institutional level —to "vote" in his church to provide time and personnel for much beyond the most casual and short-term counseling for individuals and groups. Second, the middle-class church is remarkably slow to allocate funds for supporting pastoral counseling and care for the poor and disadvantaged who cannot afford to pay a well-trained pastoral counselor.

The Free Exercise of the Pulpit

A pastor can, if he will, break through the plate-glass wall of denial and respectability through the disciplined use of preaching. Pastoral counseling as an ordered discipline in the ministry received much of its initial thrust from pastors who preached in such a way as to focus the whole counsel of God upon the intimately personal needs of their congregations. Charles Kemp has called this "life-situation" preaching. Horace

Bushnell preached on "unconscious influence" and laid clearly before people the dynamics of identification. Harry Emerson Fosdick preached on the subject of "Making Our Mischievous Consciences Behave" (*On Being a Real Person*; Harper & Brothers, 1943) and showed how we can mistake the "dictates of our own conscience" for the ultimate purposes of God to our own dis-ease.

Fosdick measured the effectiveness of his preaching by the number of individual inquirers it stimulated to seek personal counseling. He was in step with the tradition of Jonathan Edwards, who knew nothing of the later-invented invitation after the sermon. Instead, inquirers sought his personal guidance at his home. This stance toward preaching cannot be tagged as "liberal" or "conservative," therefore. Hanz Leitzman insists that Biblical preaching at its best happens as exegesis of an ancient message "connects up" with human anguish in the hearer: "A dialogue replaces the monologue of the Biblical author. I begin to speak, breaking in on a conversation with questions and answers, with my doubts and faith; and the Biblical text ceases to be a discourse belonging to a determined time; the text becomes a message resounding through history, which must answer the countless questions hurled by a humanity tormented by a growing anguish." (Quoted in Jérome Hamer, *Karl Barth*, tr. by Dominic M. Maruca, p. 165; The Newman Press, 1962.)

Yet such a free exercise of the pulpit is not possible if the pastor himself is the captive of the same denial and respectability as is his congregation. The reader can fill in his own illustrations, confessions, defeats, successes, and surprises here. The printer's page is too expensive for me to become an "exhorter" at this point. You as a reader can look closely at your own preaching and learn more. I would make only two suggestions: First, form a group of persons out of your church who have the closest contact with the private lives of the membership. They may be anyone from the most highly trained professional counselors to the people who lend money to the operator of a crossroads grocery or service station. Seek their guidance and feedback on what the recurrent human problems are and how your preaching is connecting up with these concerns. Do this informally, quietly, and with no publicity. Second, form a group of your fellow pastors into a continuing sermon preparation collegium. They could be called the "Exegetical Crew," the "Sermon Brainstormers," or some such title. Today's minister seems to function better in a group of peers.

The Redefinition of the Associate Pastor's Role

A second attempt to break through the denial and respectability barrier has been the redefinition of the role and function of the associate pastor. Congregations under the leadership of pastors who can accept another pastor as a colleague can call an associate pastor whose primary responsibilities are in the area of crisis intervention and formal counseling. This assignment of duties does not overlap at the point of both wanting to preach. The associate pastor gets his fullest satisfaction in individual counseling and group leadership.

The redefinition of the role of the associate pastor has been increasingly used by churches of several denominations all along the theological spectrum of liberalism and conservatism. One theological facet appears as churches of an extreme fundamentalist and an extreme liberal persuasion both tend to choose persons who are trained in clinical psychology or social work but have no theological training. The separation of theological inspection from the counseling done is a curious phenomenon worth studying empirically in a dissertation.

A Counseling Service in the Context of a Church

A third pattern for breaking through the barrier of denial and respectability is the establishment of a formal counseling service on the church premises. Usually this is done by the appointment of a board of advisers from the professional persons in or closely related to the congregation. The counselor is a clinically trained and experienced pastor. He does group counseling with the local congregation. Individual counseling, particularly with people who are not members of the church, is done on a fee-taking basis according to a scale of ability to pay. The use of retreats for the improvement of interpersonal relationships is also a tool of ministry.

The practicality of this arrangement is that people who are not participants in the life of the church can be helped by the church and at the same time pull their part of the financial load insofar as they are able. The possibility of the clinic or service becoming unrelated to the ongoing life is a persistent threat. Once the service and the competence of its staff are established in the confidence of the larger community, three things can happen. First, the budgeting of the church from the general operating expense may fall off. Second, if the support of the church lags, the fee-cost for service goes up and the service exists only geographically in relation to the church. It may even move to a separate building. Benevolent donors can aid and abet this process through endowment of the service. The fees and independent gifts enable the counseling service to be autonomous of the church. There are some indications that the distinctly pastoral nature of the counseling changes as the relation to the church support changes. Third, neither of these results need happen. For example, in one church that has had such a service for two years, the fees from persons not related to the church amounted to well over $12,000 for the two years. The church that will persevere until such a counseling service is firmly rooted in the community may discover that, instead of retrenchment of funds, the services can be expanded even more.

The Corporate Endeavor of Several Churches

One of the phenomena of the 1950's and 1960's was the establishment of counseling services by associations and/or councils of churches. Large associations of churches of the same denomination—such as American Baptist in Los Angeles and, in my own city of Louisville, the Catholic diocese—provided counseling assistance on an area-wide basis. The councils of churches of various communities have succeeded in establishing such counseling services. One of the most vital examples of service, teaching, and research under the support of several churches is the Virginia Institute of Pastoral Care in Richmond, Virginia. Another such example was begun under the auspices of the ministerial associations of Jeffersonville, Clarksville, and New Albany, Indiana. Gradually the church support diminished and gave out completely. As it did so, the United Fund began to fund the service modestly. Likewise the average fee charged was increased. The service began to meet more distinctly marriage counseling ministry, as such.

The weakening and collapse of many councils of churches has reduced their institutional base of support for counseling services as well as other corporate efforts of churches. The emergence of interfaith ecumenicity—Protestant, Catholic, and Jewish—shows some faint promise of a base of institutional support of the skilled pastoral counseling of persons in crises and conflicts. In the meantime, judicatories of specific denominations are making progress in providing denominational funds for pastoral counseling centers.

THEOLOGICAL ISSUES AT STAKE

Several crucial theological issues emerge in the severe ambiguity between the institutional and personal necessities of a pastoral counselor.

Town Hall or Body of Christ?

The first theological issue is the confusion of the American tradition of the town hall meeting with the Biblical perception of the church as the body of Christ at work healing its members. If, for example, a minority of a membership have a concern, a commitment of time and money, then an official board or even the majority of a church body should be left with the burden of proof to "go and do likewise." It seems alien to the nature of the church for a given group who really want to do works of mercy to have to ask permission of the rest of the body to do so.

If, however, we perceive the church as a town hall where the majority rules, such permission is certainly appropriate. The very use of the real estate itself aids and abets the plausibility of the "town hall" conception of the church. Reducing such a procedure to absurdity: it would have required that the good Samaritan should have gotten some official board's permission before he cared for the wounded man!

My contention is that the modern church is a pluralistic community. Some of the members have some concerns and other members have different ones. If good can be done without endless meetings of committees, judicatory meetings, *and without the quest for publicity,* then the church can be more nearly its true self. I know that I am in the spirit of many young persons today who simply set about doing what needs to be done. They do not wait for everyone's permission to do what is obviously the intention of God for them.

The City of Refuge and the People of God

In Num. 35:9–15 the story is told of how the Jews arranged six cities to which people who had become unrespectable by impulsive murder might flee before they themselves were hurt by others who were angered by their acts. These were sanctuary cities, much as the cathedrals of Europe were sanctuaries for offenders in their era. Today the denial and respectability needs of the well-to-do, the pious, the outwardly conforming church member are overwhelming. Many church members carry their hidden secrets and shame so well that nothing is known in the church about it until the scandal appears as disaster news in the newspaper.

Such persons apparently need a "city of refuge," a place of protective sanctuary where these issues may be arbitrated in such a way that arbitration itself neither is hindered nor causes further damage. Much marriage conflict, business malfeasance, and family inheritance struggle is of this nature.

Could it be that pastoral counseling of a very private and unheralded nature provides that kind of sanctuary or "city of refuge" for many people? I think so. Couple this with the increasing body of identifiable data in pastoral psychology to which people of all stations in life need access, and we can see why pastoral counseling as we have developed it is here to stay for some time yet. Pastoral counseling is more than the general practice of ministry today. Informed pastoral counselors have access to data and skills not available to the generalist type of pastor. The pastoral counselor must take upon himself the tension between the institutional structures of the church and the wounds that people carry hidden in their beings and between them and others, denying them in behalf of respectability.

THREE MAJOR TEMPTATIONS TO IRRESPONSIBILITY

The Temptation to Avoid Administration

As the pastor learns the tension between institutional and personal demands, he suffers three temptations. First, the pastoral counselor is tempted to avoid institutional responsibility, to disdain any administrative tasks. As Morris Taggart says, "Pastoral counselors do not appear to be terribly interested in administration, whether on the local or national scene." (*The Journal of Pastoral Care*, December 1972, pp. 219–244.) There is an emerging administrative bureaucracy among pastoral counselors and Association for Clinical Pastoral Education people, but when it comes to the nitty-gritty tackling of the administrative shot-calling by ecclesiastical establishments and the hierarchies of other health profession establishments such as the medical association, the association of hospital administrators, the administrators of the vast complex of comprehensive mental health centers and regions, we as pastors in the main are cop-outs. We will sit on our hands until somebody else does the administrative head-knocking, hard-nosed negotiation, and frank use of political power to get a job opening, a salary, etc., for the pastoral counselor to enjoy a good job, a good salary, and continue to be "not terribly interested in administration." This is, in my opinion, one of the reasons pastoral counseling does not "appear to stand high on anyone's list as an area of needs"—we are passive by temperament, training, and methodology when it comes to participating in the administrative processes which provide the logistics for adequate programs of pastoral counseling, the teaching and learning of pastoral counseling, and the support and supply of such efforts.

One can ask whether pastoral counseling is a credible alternative in the ministry today. The answer is an unqualified yes. Brute necessity requires it. Twenty years ago Liston Pope, of Yale Divinity School, predicted that pastoral counseling would pass off the scene because it was a fad. He was wrong. It is still here in greater force than ever. Pope, with all his expertise in social ethics, underestimated the need of respectable, well-to-do church members for private, personal counseling by a person educated as a clergyman. Yet pastoral counseling was brought into being by a group of dedicated and talented people. They got their expertise over and above their training in theological school. They did their counseling over and above general pastoral work, teaching, and chaplaincy work. They did their counseling in their homes, in borrowed buildings, and on their own time. Yet they proved that people want and believe in pastoral counseling as more than a brief, informal chat after a sermon or a business meeting. As such, pastoral counseling has become credible and convincing to many persons.

Yet the pastoral counselor's active participation in administration is only one of the structural factors needed to sustain pastoral counseling as a credible alternative in the ministry. Another factor is support from the churches. Churches, denominations, and ecumenical groupings of churches are too often preoccupied with the maintenance of respectability and the building of buildings that will absorb their financial resources with exorbitant interest and debts. They use a "least common denominator" approach to the populace in their teaching of the faith. As churches, they turn their heads when people's marriages are formed, threatened, or broken. They are preoccupied with programming, when people's basic meaning in life is running out on them, when they contemplate suicide, when young persons become so nauseated at the pretense in their own homes and church that they simply dose themselves with drugs or "split the scene" entirely. They prefer social chit-chat when the substantive concerns that spiritual faith itself holds for a few spontaneously becomes more than repetition of shibboleths. When religious experience becomes a matter of ecstasy church groups want to vote to exclude those enthusiasts who require new forms of worship. When retirement and old age make people a liability to the budget rather than an asset the church too often "goes after the young people" whose parents can pay. When the still quiet desperation of people erupts into psychotic episodes, the pious church people want a *Christian* psychiatrist, not having done anything to finance the salary of a Christian chaplain in a medical center where psychiatrists are trained. When these things happen, though, they may call instead upon the highly skilled pastoral counselor. Even then they carefully avoid the mention of the relation between their use of his time and his need for financial support.

The Temptation to Succumb to Disgust

The second temptation of the pastoral counselor is impatience and disgust. The tension of the ambiguities I have just described is generated not only by the humanness-in-general of the churches, their members, and their ruling elders. The tension produces anger because of the injustice wrought by silly decisions in the spending of church funds honestly given to help other people. Anger is a normal reaction to injustice. Anger that cannot constructively change its source of injustice turns to the vinegar of disgust. As one psychiatrist who takes his faith in God seriously said to me the other day: "I'll take my chances with the lions in the Roman forum rather than with the administration of a theological seminary that suspends a student whose psychiatric symptoms hurt no one and were not a social embarrassment to anyone. He simply made the mistake of believing he could confess his problem to his dean."

Disgust is, as Erik Erikson says, the negative alternative of the aged. The pastoral counselor faces the crisis between disgust and integrity long before old age. His path to integrity lies in becoming an astute administrator in his own right. Rather than succumb to disgust, he shifts to the organizational perspective, as Hiltner suggests. This requires that he mobilize his anger in a deliberate use of political power *within* the ecclesiastical establishment.

By and large, administrators of church funds have two things in common: they are concerned with the public image of their organization and they tend to respond affirmatively to the most pervasive and unremitting pressure. They easily discourage the easily disgusted! They watch for the person who will take "no" for an answer most often. Therefore, varied, unexpected, ingenious, and constantly repeated demands tend to get results. Administrators of church funds tend to expend the money wherever it is most to the advantage of their administration to spend it. Therefore, the pastoral counselor must be politically aware enough and personally courageous enough to devise counterproposals to the administration that cannot be refused. Consequently, the training of a pastoral counselor should include here-and-now learning in the case method of studying administration and human relations. (See K. R. Andrews, ed., *The Case Method of Teaching Human Relations and Administration*; Harvard University Press, 1953.)

The alternative to disgust is to apply—with integrity—the knowledge of human behavior to administrative as well as personal, family, and group dynamics. Some of the best-kept secrets of the "respectable" are here!

The Temptation to Indulge in Free-lance Greed

The third temptation of the pastoral counselor is free-lance greed. Pastoral counselors who have found themselves competent also have discovered that people are willing to pay for competence. Pastors who get disgusted are next tempted to strike out on their own. Yet this can cause a kind of parasitic declaration of independence. The pastoral counselor uses the traditional role of the pastor as a card of entry to people's confidence. Yet he accepts no responsibility to or for the corporate fellowship of believers in God. He can, with discipline, maintain a sort of anchorite or hermit relationship to the church. As T. S. Eliot said, even the anchorite in the desert alone prays in relation to the church. This *can* be a profound relationship of integrity.

On the other hand, however, the pastoral counselor can go the way that professional, free-lance evangelism went. "Loner" evangelists have in too many instances, but not all, used the rituals, persuasions, and magic of revival as a means of "base gain," fleecing people, and peddling the formulas of the gospel. The same fate awaits the pastoral counselor who turns the rituals, persuasions, and promises of help in pastoral counseling into a free-lance way to isolated opportunism. In short, professional pastoral counseling can take historical guidance from the history of professional evangelism.

Chapter 4

THEOLOGICAL CONTINUITY
AND SCIENTIFIC DISCONTINUITY

The history of pastoral counseling as a contemporary discipline for pastors was initiated by the interaction between ministers and scientists. Medical doctors (particularly psychiatrists and psychoanalysts), social workers, and psychologists are involved with many of the same persons being ministered to also by pastors. Contemporary pastoral counseling as art and science began in dialogue with these scientists, and has continued that dialogue until now.

Pastoral counseling may be said to be a systematic effort to apply inductive, clinical, and scientific method to the accepted function of the minister as he confers with persons about their personal problems and life destiny. The scientific quest assumes a hidden world that man must discover for himself. When viewed Biblically, this means that man is subduing the earth. He rejoices when its powers, forces, and substances are "subject to him." The scientific quest further assumes that these new discoveries are discontinuous with tradition and must improve upon things that are older.

On the other hand, the pastor as a theologian and as a representative of the church is committed to a heritage of faith. He knows a set of beliefs and doctrines that have been transmitted to him over the centuries. He applies the historical method—which is a science in itself, also—to his ministry to persons. The pastoral counselor, therefore, must bring things both new and old from his good treasure. A faithful pastor never settles for either the historical-theological method of inquiry or the psychological approach to human need. He works in the boundary situation between the great continuities of the "deposit of faith," on the one hand, and the seeming discontinuities of scientific discovery and theory, on the other hand. He uses both to illumine his understanding of the sufferings of people. He uses psychotherapeutic wisdom and theological wisdom to make each more meaningful. He cross-checks here-and-now empirical hypotheses and discoveries by then-and-there historical-theological wisdom of the past, and vice versa. He refuses to be enchanted with either to the exclusion of the other. When he performs this act of correlation, he takes upon himself the tension of being either understood, misunderstood, or both misunderstood and understood by scientists and theologians who prefer not to take this tension upon themselves.

An Exercise in Provocation

The point of view I have just expressed cannot be appreciated most in the abstract way I have stated it. I must deliberately cause the reader to get his anger up just a few degrees. Before the next pages are finished, some readers will tend to cry, "Foul!" Others are likely to say, "He's grinding an ax!" These are responses I actually hope to stimulate in order to dramatize the way either the reader or I can become a special pleader for one side or the other of the ambiguity involved in a pastor's use of a very popular "in" kind of therapeutic model at a given point in history.

The present scientific form of counseling known as transactional analysis and devised first by Eric Berne is at this writing of wide influence among pastoral counselors. The conflict and cooperation between Parent ego states, Adult ego states, and Child ego states is the topic of much discussion among pastoral counselors. The transactional analysis system is easily taught and learned. TA, as it is nicknamed, is much fun to apply. TA is, therefore, readily taken as "the" thing in many circles of pastoral counselors. To speak critically of TA in some groups is almost heresy. Therefore, I will do just that.

If one takes transactional analysis uncritically, he settles the stress of being a distinctly *pastoral* counselor. He becomes enamored with TA. He may forget his responsibility as a theologian and pastor. He ceases to exercise historical and theological wisdom about TA as a new form of therapy. Yet, on the other hand, other pastors uncritically reject transactional analysis with the protest that it is not Biblical or theological. They resolve their own stress on the other side of the ambiguity. They miss the flashes of insight that transactional analysis can throw upon Biblical study and theological reflection. The genuinely pastoral counselor cannot let himself get caught on either of the horns of this dilemma. He brings both TA and historical-theological-Biblical into focus, bears the tension, and brings them into dialogue with each other.

When a pastor accepts the stress of this dilemma between transactional analysis and theological understanding, as a counselor he is being uniquely pastoral. He can use the one to contribute to the other. As he does so, he sees to it that the wisdom of transactional analysis will lose some of its transience. Ancient theological truth itself can, through TA insights, be made more understandable to people who need redemption.

My exercise in provocation continues: Transactional analysis does not seem to me adequately to deal with the hard problems of sibling rivalry. A short scientific memory would inform transactional analysis with the concepts of Alfred Adler about sibling rivalry. The transactional analyst's preoccupation with parental authority can helpfully inform the TA knowledge of "sibling game structures." A longer memory of the wisdom of the Bible would call upon the Biblical understanding of conflict and cooperation between brothers—Cain and Abel, Jacob and Esau, Joseph and his brothers, the prodigal son and the elder brother, the twelve disciples, and the apostle Paul and the apostle Peter. Transactional analysis helps illumine such Biblical stories on the power structure of these individuals' relationship to their competitors and to God. Biblical wisdom can deepen transactional analysis with its observation concerning the interaction between siblings. Competition pervades American life; it is the content of many counseling sessions. Distance, cleverness, and deception—of which TA speaks much—are the fabric of competition. At its root, theologically, is the desire to be as God! The pastor, as I shall suggest later in more detail, inveterately sees a new system of psychotherapy through his own value system. He practices disciplined naïveté, however, by "bracketing in" his values long enough to learn a given approach to a counseling system in the purest form possible. Yet there comes a time when his *own* values are brought into critical activity.

The pastoral counselor's critical faculties require that he bring a knowledge of the history of counseling and a knowledge of church history, theology, and the Bible into dialogue with changing emphases in scientific approaches to counseling. A careful review of these changing emphases in pastoral counseling as it has developed over the last forty years will demonstrate the ways in which pastoral counselors have handled the tension between psychological discontinuity and theological continuity.

CHANGING EMPHASES IN PASTORAL COUNSELING

Early Intimations of the Struggle

Prescientific resources concerning the pastoral care of individuals and groups reveal intimations of a tension between the empirical application of scientific know-how and the exercise of the power of belief in God. For example, a double interpretation of the life and acts of Jesus is found in Mark 3:19–27. Jesus' friends sought to protect him, saying, "He is beside himself." The learned scribes from Jerusalem, however, applied the intricate psychological theory of demons and said, "He is possessed by Beelzebul, and by the prince of demons he casts out the demons." Jesus' friends interpreted his experience as a profound—even religious—ecstasy, whereas his enemies seem to have interpreted it in the current psychological idiom of the day—demonology.

In the Middle Ages and recurrently throughout history since then, elaborate prescientific psychological theories were propounded in the name of witchcraft. The more human experience of persons as persons, responsible to God for their behavior, was espoused by humanitarian physicians such as Phillipe Pinel. Gregory Zilboorg tells the fascinating story of this tension in his book *A History of Medical Psychology* (W. W. Norton & Company, Inc., 1967).

The full activation of the life of a religious congregation in the care of disturbed and unhappy people is found in a case record, dated 1673, from the church minutes of the Broadmead Church, Bristol, England. The congregation found one of their members "distracted, despairing, and in a state of mind and behavior that was directly opposite and contrary to the whole frame of his former way and temper." The large percentage of the church apparently wanted to have him "carried into the country for help." However, some of the church members decided to devote themselves completely to his care, called upon the physician in the community to help them, and stayed by him until he was well and able to go forth about his business in the city, working as a salesman. (The full text of this case is recorded in my book *Protestant Pastoral Counseling,* pp. 131–138; The Westminster Press, 1962.)

The group perceived that "the Lord was pleased to have us use outward means," and they believed that he would direct them to these means and "bless the means." This small group of people kept the tension going between the use of prayer before God, the fellowship and the communion of a group of fellow Christians on the one hand, and the use of scientific means on the other hand. They did not make an either-or of prayer and scientific means. They took the tension upon themselves. The tension is described vividly in that they said that what they had to listen to from the disturbed person "made the hearts of all that heard it to ache, and the hairs of their heads, as it were, to stand on end: and their spirits to be so pressed thereby hardly able to contain or to be in the room to hear it." Nor did the small group wait for a "town hall" majority of the congregation to okay their words of love. They just did what God prompted them to do.

Seward Hiltner, in his book *Preface to Pastoral Theology* (pp. 72–85; Abingdon Press, 1958), describes the work of a pastor, Ichabod S. Spencer, a Presbyterian minister who recorded careful sketches of his pastoral work done in the years prior to 1851–1853. Spencer showed real acumen for observing and recording his data. He used an empirical method of observation. At the same time he thought seriously as a theologian. He reflects the tension that a genuinely pastoral counselor has to bear. He was honest when he did not know what to do. He advocated experimental religion. He believed that a message is more than a proclamation. Spencer himself was a man of deep piety and had a "sharp pietistic focus on religion as a thing apart." He nevertheless reflected upon and improved his work through the process of writing sketches about what he was doing. He searched empirically for signs of improvement and depended upon a psychological process whether he called it that or not. One characteristic of Spencer's pastoral method remains to this day in pastoral counseling as we know it: careful recording of the results of one's work. This is the beginning of a scientific method in pastoral counseling, regardless of who does it.

Pastoral Counseling as the Facilitation of Insight

At best, the pastor, the priest, the rabbi—however entitled—has historically been perceived by the wisdom literature of the Judeo-Christian tradition as "a man of understanding." The *tebunah*, in the Old Testament, is a man of perception. He has the capacity to discern between the things that matter and the things that do not matter. The *tebunah* has insight into the deep purposes or plans in man's mind. As Prov. 20:5 states it, "The purpose in a man's mind is like deep water, but a man of understanding will draw it out." Being such a man of understanding calls for empathy with other people's weaknesses, insight into one's own besetting weaknesses, and the capacity to deal gently with the ignorant and the wayward. (Heb. 4:14 to 5:3.) The function of the minister as "a man of understanding" and as a gentle and compassionate confessor is an unbroken line of historical and theological continuity. Bad practice and neglect of the function of the *tebunah* obscures but does not destroy this continuous ministry of pastors, priests, and rabbis.

Scientific explorers into the depths of man's being began to exert influence upon pastoral counselors in the late 1920's and early 1930's. Rollo May, in his book *The Art of Counseling* (Abingdon-Cokesbury Press, 1939), drew heavily upon the works of Alfred Adler, Sigmund Freud, C. G. Jung, Otto Rank, and J. B. Rhine in interpreting what he calls the key to the counseling process. He says that "the counselor works basically through the process of empathy. Both he and the counselee are taken out of themselves and become merged in a common psychic entity" (*ibid.*, p. 81). An almost telepathic understanding is derived through participation in depth with a counselee.

In a similar vein, Seward Hiltner reflects the goal of pastoral counseling as the achievement of insight through a dynamic relationship to the counselee. He says that "the generic aim of counseling is new insight, with proof in action. That is, if a person is troubled about his situation or some aspect of it and seeks a helper through counseling, the end which all such professional helpers have in common is to aid the person to get a sufficiently clear view of his situation, with the conflicting trends and pulls and motives and ideals and desires, that he may then see his situation in a freer. clearer, more objective way and consequently be able to act in a similar new fashion." (Seward Hiltner, *Pastoral Counseling*, p. 95; Abingdon-Cokesbury Press, 1949.) The succeeding pages of Hiltner's book reflect Hiltner's seriousness in bringing the point of view of depth psychologists into focus with the heritage of the Christian ministry.

Freud states the goals of insight therapy most succinctly in his first axiom of therapy. The axiom assumes unconscious mental processes. The purpose of therapy is the bringing of the unconscious into the consciousness which provides meaning for one's senseless behavior. When this meaning is seen, worked through, accepted, and genuinely understood, the axiom assumes that the symptoms will vanish. Somewhat less influential upon pastoral counselors was the work of the Gestalt psychologists such as Köhler, Koffka, and Wertheimer, who in various ways were saying that certain occurrences in human experience make sense while others fail to do so. Insight occurs when otherwise senseless experiences connect up in such a way that they are genuinely understood and assimilated into the productive thinking and behavior of a person. One's values are the sense or understanding he has of the world of facts around him. (See Wolfgang Köhler, *The Place of Value in a World of Facts*; Liveright Publishing Corporation, 1938.)

The emphasis on insight and understanding penetrated pastoral counseling practice in the years from 1939 to 1963 in more than a passing manner. The positive contribution that insight therapy made was threefold: (1) Forgiveness through the confession of sin is authentic and powerful only when accompanied by genuine understanding, insight, and acceptance on the part of both the counselor and the counselee. (2) Such understanding called for pastors to develop creative listening as a technique in counseling. Listening means to hear what the person says, to let the person say it, and to facilitate the process of their saying it. Listening means using one's eyes to appreciate the nonverbal communication attending the words. (3) The achievement of insight represents a return of repressed memories as they are related to the present feelings of a person, the expression of ambivalent feelings, and the experience of self-acceptance in the face of unacceptable feelings. Faith is the acceptance of the self as worthy before God, even though it is unacceptable to oneself. Such faith is a ground to stand upon before God to become the fulfilled person God intends one to be.

The techniques of implementing insight therapy reached a zenith in the work of Carl Rogers. He became intensely influential on pastoral counseling with the publication of his book *Counseling and Psychotherapy* (Houghton Mifflin Company, 1942).

The person who carried the assimilation of insight therapy's durable results into theology was David Roberts. His book *Psychotherapy and a Christian View of Man* (Charles Scribner's Sons, 1950) described the difference between static and dynamic salvation and faith. He kept our generation of pastoral counselors' thinking in dialogue with our heritage as we struggled to learn the complexities of insight therapy.

I myself disciplined myself in the original documents and concepts, methodology, and personal self-examination of psychoanalysis. At the same time, I reexamined my own Biblical heritage and tested the discoveries I made in personal therapy with my adult learning of the Scriptures. Freud himself was an astute and serious student of the Old Testament. My own encounter with the Old and New Testaments began after I was twenty years of age. Consequently, the Bible has never been a book of magic to me, but a reservoir for my becoming a "man of understanding." I state these autobiographical comments to show where my own "gut level" involvement with the ambiguities of insight therapy and the issues of sin and salvation began and has continued.

It would be easy enough for a pastor, a priest, or a rabbi to be carried away with the mysteries of insight therapy and to overlook the ethical levels of insight that Christian ethics can inform. The pastoral counselor can keep his theological bearings or locations by distinguishing between different ethical qualities of insight. *Ascetic insight,* for example, is that quality of understanding in which a person sees problems of aggression, passion, etc., but simply uses all his energies in controlling himself. *Fatalistic insight* is that kind in which a person *sees* his problems, but feels impotent and refuses to accept any responsibility for doing anything about them. A third quality of insight would be a *Machiavellian insight* in which the person uses his insight, not to move toward a higher level of maturity or competence, but to take advantage of the people around him on a deceptive basis. From an ethical point of view, the most desirable kind of insight is that which *both* discovers freedom of action for the person himself and is an instrument with which the person brings release from bondage to those around him. He seeks to alleviate their sufferings even as his have been alleviated for him. He learns not only to experience empathy from a counselor but also to express empathy toward others.

Pastoral Counseling as Interpersonal Interaction

In the early to middle 1950's, pastoral counseling emphasized listening, empathy, and responsive counseling to such an extent that a whole generation of exceptionally passive pastors was produced. Pastoral counseling developed as a passive art after the medical model in which people were expected to "ask for help" before they got it. In the counseling process itself, reflective, understanding, and insight-producing responses were "okay"; evaluative, confrontational, and interpretive responses were "not okay."

Harry Stack Sullivan and Martin Buber began to change the passive emphasis to a more active one. Instead of interpreting the interview as a sort of one-way communication system, Sullivan saw it as primarily vocal communication in a two-group. The purpose of insight was maintained but defined much more specifically as that of "elucidating *characteristic patterns of living* of the counselee. The particular patterns that are troublesome or valuable would be sorted out in such a way that the counselee would derive benefit" (Harry Stack Sullivan, *The Psychiatric Interview,* p. 4; W. W. Norton & Company, Inc., 1954). In order to understand these characteristic patterns of living, the counselor must get acquainted with what sort of person the total being of his counselee is. Distortion of his perception of the person must be clarified. Genuine benefit from the interviews must be derived. The counselor, therefore, is not just a passive listener and sounding board. Rather, he is a *participant-observer*. He plays a very active role, "not to show that he is smart or that he is skeptical, but literally to make sure that he knows what he is being told." Being clearly understood benefits the counselee. He knows that the counselor cares enough "to discover exactly what is meant." Sullivan says, "And what a relief it is to him to discover that his true meaning is anything but what he at first says, and that he is at last, at long last, uncovering some conventional self-deception that he has been pulling on himself for years." (*Ibid.*, p. 21.)

Sullivan and his followers took the tension of theological and philosophical inquiry upon themselves. They sought out the help of the Jewish philosopher Martin Buber. In Buber's poetic volume, *I and Thou* (Charles Scribner's Sons, 2d ed., 1958), he moved both interpersonal psychiatry and pastoral counseling into a realm of I-Thou relationships as over against I-It relationships. Thus, counseling becomes a "meeting" of "thou's" in which there is both distance and relation, tenderness and objectivity, understanding and mystery, frank appreciation of each other and serious independence of each other.

The penetration of this new emphasis in pastoral counseling was expressed by Carroll A. Wise in his book *Pastoral Counseling: Its Theory and Practice* (Harper & Brothers, 1951). He said that "counseling is essentially communication and as such is a two-directional process. It is not what the counselor does to or for the counselee that is important; the important thing is what happens between them" (p. 11). Wise does not disavow insight as a goal in counseling, but points out that "explanation is impotent to change personality" (p. 119). He also emphasizes the levels of insight, but there is a shift of emphasis to the primacy of the person, what communication means, the satisfaction of needs, the acceptance of one's strengths as well as the realization of one's limitations.

In my own book *Protestant Pastoral Counseling*, I made conscious use of Sullivan's characteristic patterns of living in a chapter entitled "Pastoral Counseling as Self-encounter." The pastor himself has a characteristic pattern of living which either gears in with or abrasively creates friction with another person. Yet in that book I sought to appreciate the scientific discontinuity created by the emphases of Sullivan and also to interpret the pastoral counseling relationship in terms of the sovereignty of God before which both the counselor and the counselee stand as being more distinctly human than otherwise, as Sullivan would put it. Also, I interpreted the counseling process in relation to the life of the community of the church to which the pastor is related and to which he seeks to relate the counselee. The work of the Holy Spirit who is the one who has come alongside, the Paraclete, the Counselor of both the person seeking help and the one seeking to help him, I see as the nonverbal Presence in counseling. The more or less kenotic, or incarnational, approaches to pastoral counseling of the earliest eras seemed to me at that time to need some correction. Therefore, I emphasized the role of the demonic in human life which is set in motion by idolatrous construction. The Spirit of God liberates the counselee and counselor from the power of idolatry.

The heavy weight of the ambiguity between the interaction psychologies of Sullivan and others, on the one hand, and the theological heritage of the Christian faith, on the other hand, was nobly borne in this era by the theologian Paul Tillich. He took up the serious questions of psychotherapy and correlated them with "the Protestant principle." According to his affirmation, the Protestant principle was the refusal to place anything relative in the position of the absolute, a process that he called absolutizing the relative. He distinguished between pathological anxiety and existential anxiety. The former was a clinical syndrome, but the latter is the basic condition of all persons. He exercised massive influence upon psychotherapists of all persuasions, and was open to dialogue with them.

However, the advent of Vatican II has demonstrated that many of the principles that we hitherto perceived as Protestant principles are not our private possession at all. As we stood on the verge of the counter-culture explosion in 1963, however, these distinctions were very important. Tillich called the resistance to idolatry the "Protestant principle." Hence I entitled my work *Protestant Pastoral Counseling,* a title which itself now points to a certain obsolescence. We now enter a kind of theological era that affirms the basic humanity of all people as being more distinctly alike than they are different. This kernel of wisdom will probably be the prophetic insight for which we are most indebted to Harry Stack Sullivan. As William James said, "There is not much difference between human beings, but what little there is seems to matter very much to each of us."

Power-oriented Pastoral Counseling

The assassination of John F. Kennedy is as good a historical event as any with which to mark the beginning of the social upheaval to which we are now, eleven years later, still trying to get accustomed. For the lack of a better name, this upheaval has been called the emergence of the counter culture. A variety of events seem to have set it into motion and to have given it energy. The assassinations not only of John F. Kennedy but also of Robert Kennedy and of Martin Luther King, and the attempted assassination of George Wallace, have surfaced a motif of violence in the civilian life of America. The ambiguities of the Vietnam war have produced four college generations of persons who have been alternately apathetic and violent. They have been introduced to indecision as a way of life at both the national and the personal levels. The emergence of "the executive" as the single-handed decision maker who leaves his followers either in impotence because of the power he preempts or in indecision because of his fear of the power he has, or both, has created a power-conscious population. Contemporary power consciousness is something more than social climbing. The indecision created by the draft and the Vietnam war power consciousness has produced a childlike, Eden-like sense of timelessness and un-committedness in great segments of our population. Indecision and uncommittedness are symptomatic of a feeling of power-lessness or impotence. These attitudes are among all age groups and are simply more noticeable among young persons.

Out of the sense of impotence has emerged an array of secular types of counseling which are built upon what I would call power-impotence models of the therapeutic proc-ess. They emphasize the ways in which distance is maintained through deception. These ways are called games-structures. These forms of therapy emphasize the need for openness and intimacy and offset the feeling of impotence in large, bureau-cratic structures with the feeling of power in small groups. Power-impotence models of counseling can be classified under two large headings: transactional analysis and sensitivity training.

Transactional analysis emphasizes the ways that "witch messages" from one's continuing (not necessarily past) pa-rental ego state immobilize the spontaneity and creativity of one's adult state by pushing a person back into an unaccept-able or "not-okay" child state. The objective of the therapy seems to be the development of a realistic Parent ego state, an operative Adult ego state, and a joyous and nondeceptive Child ego state. However, the forces of fear and feelings of impotence produce a game-structure that thrives on distance and deception. The transactional analyst, therefore, is to re-move the fear and impotence by creating an atmosphere of permission and personal power whereby the games can be called off and seen clearly by the adult state for what they really are. Then, it is hoped, a feeling of intimacy and self-confidence is engendered. Consequently, with intimacy and a sense of potency or self-confidence as its goals, transactional analysis has taken the form of group therapy. Group therapy has gone far toward replacing one-to-one counseling; nevertheless, TA insights are used widely in individual counseling as well.

Some of the same kinds of objectives, with a different methodology, characterize the sensitivity training movement which has its theoretical roots in the psychology of Abraham Maslow. (Abraham Maslow, *Toward a Psychology of Being*; D. Van Nostrand Company, Inc., 1968.) Maslow placed the maximum weight of his psychology upon the basic potentials of people rather than upon the crippling liabilities that cause them to feel different from others and weak in their own eyes. The human potential movement has, therefore, moved upon the assumptions of the natural expansion of human awareness, the increase of sensitivity to the positive resources of life for creative living. The development of the element of trust and closeness in small groups which are set within a society where distance and role-playing keep people from realizing the depths of their relationships to one another.

One of the great challenges that both the transactional analysts and the sensitivity therapists have brought to pastoral counseling, as such, is to question the viability of the emphasis that we have placed upon role performance. Pastoral counseling of the 1950's and 1960's was much preoccupied with the issues of what the role of the pastor is as over against the role of the psychologist, psychiatrist, etc. Furthermore, persons with an ingrained conception of the ministry as a uniquely ordained calling tended to fall into the *Zeitgeist* of sociological role theory and role-playing to such an extent that the distinctly existential being-cognition awareness of life as function rather than role was obscured.

From a theological point of view these power-oriented challenges to the role structure of our life as a people raised the issue of our interpretation of our relationship to God as a parent as over against us as children of God. Is the substance of religion a feeling of absolute dependence? Or, in these difficult times, is this interpretation simply a perpetuation of people's feelings of impotence and distance at a time when personal self-confidence, decisiveness, and adult responsibility are in very short supply? Even more than this, the feeling of intimacy in co-laboring with God and communion through prayer is at itself at low ebb as compared with the high tides of the feelings of desolation, desertion, indecisiveness, and credibility gaps between people and their parent figures.

Such power-oriented approaches to pastoral counseling have also challenged pastoral counselors at the point of our lack of involvement in social action. Persons like Robert Bonthius insist that pastoral counseling and pastoral care more generally should become politicized. By this he means that we should take more seriously the responsibility we have to exercise political power and social processes to alleviate some of the great social ills that beset people. Apart from this, he feels, we are simply snatching coals from the burning by individual counseling with persons who are victims of these great systems that render them impotent, helpless, "flayed and cast down" like sheep without a shepherd.

Bonthius' point of view must be tempered with the wisdom of what Halmos calls "micro-sociology." Halmos says that, in the past, social action interests were prompted by political disaffection, doubt, and searching. In the present, however, "the dominant motive seems to be personal unhappiness about concrete human relationships" (Paul Halmos, *The Faith of the Counsellors,* p. 26; Schocken Books, Inc., 1966). The pastoral counselor sees the individual counselee, family, or small group as a microscopic specimen of all of society. Here he finds the specific pathologies that need changing en masse. The principles of preventive pastoral counseling have been devised to reshape the large structures of society, to find a target for the attack on social evils. It is more tedious and less dramatic than political image-building as a means of social change. My own conviction is that it is more accurate. Yet, once the target has been found as a large social evil, mass action must be mobilized.

Up to this time the field of pastoral counseling has been involved in rather intense political activity and social change

in establishing its own identity as a credible source of help
and encouragement to people. However, at the time of this
writing, pastoral counseling has reached a stage of acceptance
that would not have been dreamed of twenty years ago. The
position that it has in theological education, in counseling
services throughout the country, and in the minds of more
people than there are trained pastoral counselors to serve,
has made it a part of the Establishment. Pastoral counselors
in great numbers are mature enough and have enough influence to exercise some of the political power for which
Bonthius is calling. Our own needs for role security, economic
affluence, and overidentification with prestige groups may
shackle us as they have shackled both medical doctors and
lawyers when it comes to exercising power in behalf of
minority groups: the poor and the people who have chosen
to learn about life in some other avenue of learning than the
prestige system of the schools, colleges, and universities.

Therefore, the development of pastoral counselors in the
next twenty years, it seems to me, calls for a more functional
and less role-oriented approach to people. The pastoral counseling of the future must emphasize the informal tools of
serving people and be less preoccupied with the highly
structured and method-actor approaches that have preoccupied us in the past twenty years. For example, in training
pastoral counselors we need more varied methods of report-
ing than the monotonous verbatim. We need case records of
power struggles in communities as well as of inner personal
stresses of individuals. In short, pastors must move toward
people as individuals and populaces. They must explore the
hazards and opportunities of the marketplace type of counseling and care. They must ask for a part of the action in
social change efforts. They must not be squeamish about the
use of political power.

Family Therapy and Pastoral Counseling

The impact of psychoanalysis brought with it the issues of
sexuality and the life of love. The maxim of Freud was that

the issues of life are *Lieben und Arbeiten,* "love and work." Pastoral counseling has through the centuries and into the present been deeply related to the family. Consequently, Freud set into motion the scientific quest for freeing persons from impediments to the ability to be creative because of sexual ignorance, wrong habituation, and value distortions. The rapid publication of the Kinsey reports on human sexuality, the later reports of the Masters and Johnson studies of the human sexual response opened the way for a sexual revolution. The revolution focused attention on the therapy, not just of the sexual life of persons, but the whole family constellation.

The emphasis in counseling took a turn toward the therapy of the family as a total unit. One of the pioneers in this kind of therapy was Nathan Ackerman. He says that wholeness of life "is not a static quality in the private possession of anyone. It is not self-sustaining. It can be maintained by continuous exertion and with the emotional togetherness and support of others." The generative source of this is the family. (Nathan Ackerman, *The Psychodynamics of Family Life,* p. 7; Basic Books, Inc., 1958.) Therefore, Ackerman decided to treat the family as a total unit and not as individuals isolated from one another.

This challenged a sacred commitment of keeping the therapy of an individual separate from the interaction of the other family members. It moved therapeutic efforts of scientific therapists nearer to the natural situation of the pastor. By nature of his involvement with the whole family, the pastor by necessity is involved with the nuclear family and even the continuity of generations within a family. I can recall the unrealism I felt as a pastor in trying to apply purely individual counseling procedures to the interacting complexities of the demands of from one to a dozen family members! The reality of the pastoral situation by its nature involves the whole family. The responsibility that is inherently the pastor's has been enriched and informed by the work of Nathan Ackerman, Virginia Satir, David Mace, Evelyn Duvall, and others.

On the other hand, we pastors have a good tradition of our own in attending to family counseling. The work of Roy Burkhart in the full-guidance church concept at First Community Church in Columbus, Ohio, is still an experiment to study and emulate. He sought to give guidance to persons at every crucial turning in life from birth to death. Furthermore, since 80 to 90 percent of persons marrying seek a minister to perform the ceremony, much attention has been paid to premarital counseling. The most serious volume on this is Aaron Rutledge's *Pre-marital Counseling* (Schenkman Publishing Company, Inc., 1966). More popular pamphlets on the subject have been written by Granger Westberg and myself.

Since the counterrevolution, however, social upheavals of great magnitude have made most writing on this subject and practices concerning it out of date. Increasing numbers of persons are living together without marriage. Others are making trial periods of living together a form of preparation for marriage, in their own thinking and practice. The advent of contraceptive pills and legalized abortion has made these alternatives both possible and plausible. Increasing public sentiment is "for" the limited marital contract and individuals frankly say so to pastors. The traditional vow "until death do us part" is either contested, taken with mental reservation, or entirely omitted in many marriage ceremonies. Women's liberation has a pervasive influence that radically changes the neat assumptions of specific roles for men and women. Nena and George O'Neill's *Open Marriage, A New Life Style for Couples* (M. Evans and Company, Inc., 1971) summarizes the kind of new perspective on marriage that is being adopted by many persons in more than just the earlier age groups. David R. Mace has written a book entitled *The Christian Response to the Sexual Revolution* (Abingdon Press, 1970); but pastoral counselors have not yet had the courage to write down and espouse organized points of view on the care of families at the point of marital union in the face of the sexual revolution. At the time of this writing, all that pastors have written on premarital counseling is obsolete.

But pastors are increasingly turning to "growth groups," such as those suggested by Howard Clinebell in *The People Dynamic,* to encourage and counsel family groups. Howard and Charlotte Clinebell's book *The Intimate Marriage* (Harper & Row, Publishers, Inc., 1970) is widely used to bring much of the realignment of the relationships between husbands and wives into a more equalitarian or open marriage.

The sociological changes mentioned here are not merely happening of themselves. They are being taught and programmed by enthusiasts. The bandwagon response of ministers, the passive acceptance of the changes by ministers, and the compulsive arm-waving opposition by some ministers are the three prevailing options being popularly utilized by ministers. The use of the "method of correlation" by ministers to assess these changes is still in the technical journals and at the talking stage. We are without vocal leadership to meet the issues of the sexual revolution squarely. The work of the Clinebells is our most viable option, but it does not come to grips with the Biblical and theological issues at stake in the face of the historical teachings of the churches. Whoever takes this tension upon himself has his work cut out for him. It could be a lifework, and I look to young men still in graduate school at this writing to do this well.

Reality- and Behavior-centered Pastoral Counseling

Decision-making and behavior modification are the issues that challenge the achievement of insight and the exercise of personal competence or power of being. One naïve assumption of some insight therapy is that if a person *sees* what a problem is, he will automatically do something about it of a constructive nature. This is not necessarily so. Nor is it so that if a person feels potent enough to make a decision about what he is going to do, inevitably the decision will be translated into action.

From the scientific community, therefore, has come a twin emphasis on strengthening the power of a person to make a decision by representing reality to him and developing a pattern of collaboration with him in which both the counselor and the counselee see to it that the decisions are translated into observable behavior. The reality therapy approaches of William Glasser and the behavior modification approaches of increasing numbers of clinical psychologists today represent a twin emphasis that corrects the unwarranted reliance upon insight. These types of therapy seem to be new and discontinuous with other kinds of treatment. Yet it was Otto Rank, the psychoanalyst who studied under Freud, who thirty years ago developed a corrective for classical psychoanalytic insight therapy. He called it "will therapy." His two books, *Will Therapy* and *Truth and Reality* (published in one volume by Alfred A. Knopf, Inc., 1945), are early expressions of contemporary reality therapy and behavior modification.

A longer memory would turn to the theology of Søren Kierkegaard in his deceptively simple little book *Purity of Heart: To Will One Thing* (Harper Torchbook). The thrust of his appeal was to emphasize the power of, and responsibility for, decision resident in the human being. Furthermore, the Jewish faith has relied upon ritual as a form of behavior modification for more centuries than the Christian faith has known. Consequently, the behavior patterns laid out in the law of Moses are looked upon by Jesus not as something that should be destroyed but rather as something to be fulfilled.

The private rituals that are used by many counselees who come to pastoral counselors today are a challenge to the erosion of great religious ritual in our day. Halmuth Schaefer and Patrick Martin in their book *Behavioral Therapy* (Mc-Graw-Hill Book Co., Inc., 1969) have three intriguing chapters on treating odd behaviors. These behaviors are nonsensical types of behavior that raise the individual's nuisance value in the open community. Schaefer and Martin suggest habit modification therapy that extinguishes one kind of behavior and sets in motion a more acceptable kind of ritual. Rewards and deprivations are used as techniques of motivation for change. One whole chapter, for example, is devoted to treating undesirable eating behavior. As I read this chapter I could not help recalling Old Testament food laws and the way in which rewards and deprivations were used as motivations for maintaining acceptable eating habits among the Jews. When one "free associates" on this idea, immediately the elaborate secular dieting and weight-watching concerns of the American people also come to mind.

Yet more profound than undesirable eating behaviors is the total pattern of stress under which persons live that causes them not only to be bothered by undesirable eating behaviors but also to be overwhelmed by fatigue, compulsion to work, and inability to sleep.

I return to my earlier theme: the pastoral counselor is not an eclecticist picking and choosing from this, that, and the other system of therapy. Nor is he a methodological purist who sells out his sense of history and buys into one particular kind of therapy. The pastoral counselor has both a short memory and a long memory. He has a clear knowledge of the history of the interaction of pastoral counseling with changing emphases in psychotherapy. This is a short memory. He has a long memory of history also in that he is constantly correlating the wisdom of the Hebrew-Christian tradition with what he hears and sees going on among psychotherapists and their patients. He himself takes his stand with the Hebrew-Christian tradition and commits himself to probe each changing emphasis and corrective in psychotherapy for ways in which it enables him to articulate spiritual wisdom and direction to the people with whom he counsels. Nor is he simply a translator of ancient Biblical and theological truths into the most recent psychological and/or psychotherapeutic idiom. To the contrary, the pastoral counselor is a constructive critic of both the eroded religious wisdom and the seemingly new forms of therapy. He maintains his identity as a *tebunah*, "a man of understanding," who is able to bring things both new and old out of his good treasure. He is a wise and compassionate confessor, a "gadfly" provocateur, spiritual director, fellow traveler between life and death. He is an advocate in arenas of social injustice, and takes seriously the model of social activist—advocate—and a healer of hurting ideas and behaviors. In short, the pastoral counselor is a contemporary theologian at work with "the living human documents" of suffering people to whom he can extend his care or who reach out for his care. He is a person who is on speaking terms with God and has taken the time and the energy to discipline himself in the body of data that describes mankind's dealings with God throughout history.

Chapter 5

THE PROFESSIONAL
AND THE CHARISMATIC

A recurrent source of tension within the ministry throughout history has been the stress generated by the need of ministers to be disciplined, educated, and appropriately certified people, on the one hand, and their need to feel that the ministry is the free gift of God, unmerited by them, and a treasure which they hold in the earthen vessels of their humanity. An Amos could say that he was neither a prophet nor a son of a prophet, and yet he could initiate a prophetic movement that still is at work in the world. A Paul could say that he had been disciplined and trained in the law as a Pharisee of the Pharisees. He could also say that he had received his commission as an apostle not from men but from God.

The training of ministers among Christians in seminaries was a Roman Catholic innovation. Among Protestants the theological seminary or theological school came into being because German Pietists felt that universities failed to participate in the spiritual formation of ministers and did not equip them for what they had to do practically and spiritually. The first Protestant theological seminary was founded by the Lutherans in 1690 in Riddaghausen, Germany.

In colonial America there was a shortage of certified and

approved ministers. Universities such as Harvard and Prince-
ton had the requirement of developing a trained ministry
built into their charters. But, a break away from universities
began in America too. In the early part of the nineteenth
century, seminaries began to be founded. By mid-century
there were over fifty. (Glenn Hinson, "The Spiritual Formation of the Minister as a Person," *Review and Expositor,*
Vol. LXX, No. 1, 1973, p. 79.)

The frontier of America moved westward, and the push
of the Great Awakening raised up men to preach who had
none of the benefits of formal education. A division developed
among Christians over the reliability and certification of such
uneducated preachers. The Cumberland Presbyterians broke
away, for example, from main-line Presbyterianism over this
issue: "Is the ministry of the word only to be performed by
the educated or is it also a gift that can be performed by the
'called' and those so gifted?" Some denominations such as the
Southern Baptist straddled the issue by saying that both
could perform the work of ministry and that education would
not be prerequisite to ordination. Yet they have six of the
largest seminaries in the country today. Consequently, social
conflict and stress is the normal state of affairs, not between
the liberal and the conservative, but between the educated
and the uneducated Southern Baptist ministers.

More recently, however, the tension among clergymen has
been intensified on a much broader canvas than the point-
counterpoint arguments within denominations. This tension
is between and among contending perceptions of ministry
held by educated ministers, however. Is the ministry one
for which men are overeducated? Is Charles Prestwood right?
He says that "nothing in the experience of the minister-in-
training prepares him for the fact that the profession is
essentially a menial, impotent one" (Charles Prestwood, *A
New Breed of Clergy,* p. 79; Wm. B. Eerdman's Publishing
Company, 1972). His "new breed" is that group of ministers
who seek to renegotiate this menial impotence by developing
a sense of identity as *professional* persons.

Does theological education actually produce a *functioning* professional person? Does the average minister see himself as a professional person or does he see himself as an amateur? Especially is this true in the function of pastoral counseling. Pastoral counseling as a discipline has developed highly supervised forms of training in clinical pastoral education. This is called "professional education for ministry." The Association for Clinical Pastoral Education, the American Association of Pastoral Counselors, and the Academy of Parish Ministers have all three opted for a conception of the minister as a professional. Other professional persons in clinical psychology, psychiatry, and social work have reminded us, however, that we have a distinctly charismatic identity to fulfill. Jerome D. Frank, in his book *Persuasion and Healing* (The Johns Hopkins Press, 1961), Ari Kiev, in *Magic, Faith and Healing* (The Free Press of Glencoe, Inc., 1964), and Jan Ehrenwald, in his book *Psychotherapy: Myth and Method* all insist that there is a charismatic quality to any effective counseling and healing. They say that the person who performs the profession must exercise belief, the power of ritual, and a sort of conservative magic if he is to be credible. Likewise, Paul Pruyser, in his articles (as was mentioned in Chapter 3), says that the minister's intuitive response to the right of taking initiative and his perception of God's permission to convey a pastoral blessing are essential to his profession. He points out the uniqueness of the minister as counselor and man of understanding as being unabashedly charismatic and filled with confidence in this calling.

Therefore, my hypothesis is that both the professional and charismatic dimensions of our identity as pastoral counseling are inherent to the task when rightly performed. In this chapter we shall explore the meaning of, first, the professional dimension of ministry; and, second, the charismatic dimension of ministry; at the same time we shall note their paradoxical tension in relatedness.

The Professional Competence of
the Pastoral Counselor

In spite of all the limitations and ambiguities present in the role and function of the pastor, the priest, or the rabbi, he nevertheless has much individual freedom to develop his work as a counselor in its disciplined and professional connotations. Not only has he a call to the ministry but his call implies a discipline and a sense of profession that are important to his identity as a counselor.

As Daniel Jenkins says, we have been too reluctant to understand and accept the professional dimensions of the work of the minister. Enough has been said in this book about the responsibility of a pastor to God, about the involvement of the pastor with his church insofar as he functions as a counselor, and about the distinctly commercial aspects of his role to dispel any of the more popular connotations that surround the word "professional." Nevertheless, this word needs clarification in the sense that it applies to the work of the pastor as counselor. What do we mean by "professional"?

Defining a Profession

In Morris L. Cogan's "The Problem of Defining a Profession" (*The Annals of the American Academy of Political and Social Science*, January 1955, pp. 105–117), one is painfully disappointed in the nebulous discussion of the ministry's ethical bases for professional identity and action. But one is genuinely helped by Cogan's own definition of a profession, in another article: "A profession is a vocation whose practice is founded upon an understanding of the theoretical structure of some department of learning or science, and upon the abilities accompanying such understanding. This understanding and these abilities are applied to the practical affairs of man. The practices of the profession are modified by the knowledge of a generalized nature and by the accumulated wisdom and experience of mankind, which serve to correct the errors of specialism. The profession, serving the vital needs of man, considers first its ethical imperative to be altruistic service to the client." (Morris L. Cogan, "Toward a Definition of Profession," *Harvard Educational Review*, Vol. XXIII, Winter 1953, pp. 35–50.) Furthermore, Cogan's summary of the literature on the topic in the sixfold criteria of Abraham Flexner in 1915 serves as an excellent guide for the minister's understanding of himself as a disciplined as well as called servant of God: "(1) Intellectual operations coupled with large individual responsibilities, (2) raw materials drawn from science and learning, (3) practical application, (4) an educationally communicable technique, (5) tendency toward self-organization and (6) increasing altruistic motivation." (Abraham Flexner, "Is Social Work a Profession?" *School and Society*, Vol. I, June 26, 1915, p. 904.)

A study of professional competence as it is related to quackery and charlatanism has been made by William J. Goode. With a clear sense of history, he outlines the characteristics of a profession in his article "Encroachment, Charlatanism, and the Emerging Profession" (*American Sociological Review*, December 1960, Vol. XXV, No. 6, pp. 902–933). He aptly observes that "in the process of institutionalization the most severe skirmishes would occur between the new profession and the occupation closest to it in substantive and clientele interest." He also points to the history of some professions in which rival training organizations using different standards limit the profession's growth through internal competition. Finally, Goode identifies the historically constant factors in the emergence of a new profession: (1) The profession determines its own standards of education and training. (2) The student goes through a more far-reaching adult socialization than the learner in other occupations. (3) Professional practice is often legally reorganized by some form of licensure. (4) Licensing and admissions boards are manned by members of the profession. (5) The legislation concerned with the profession is shaped by the profession. (6) The occupation gains in income, power, and prestige ranking and can demand higher caliber students. (7) The practitioner is relatively free of lay evaluation and control. (8) The norms of practice enforced by the profession are more stringent than legal controls. (9) Members are more strongly identified and affiliated with the profession than are members of other occupations with theirs. (10) The profession is more likely to be a terminal occupation. Members do not care to leave it, and a higher proportion assert that if they had it to do over, they would again choose this type of work.

We as ministers become too moralistic when we use the word "professional" as if it were an obnoxious thing. We need to measure our own work as ministers, especially in the context of the local ministerial association, by the following standards:

In the first place, the pastoral counselor is professional in the sense that he has committed all his time to the work of being a pastor. He has disentangled himself from other pursuits. He thrusts himself upon all the risks involved in being dependent upon the church, school, hospital, the comprehensive mental health center, the board of a pastoral counseling center and the role of its ministry for his economic support and his identity as a person. This has called for singular decisiveness on his part. If he remains in the ministry and functions competently, this commitment of his time thrusts upon him the responsibility of developing a clear-cut sense of purpose and identity. As Nelson Foote and Leonard Cottrell have said, "There is an inseparable relationship between identity and interpersonal competence." This particularly applies to the more distinctly professional aspects of being a minister.

In the second place, interpersonal competence is characteristic of the ministry as a profession. Nelson Foote and Leonard Cottrell aptly describe several aspects of interpersonal competence. These can be applied to the work of the pastor as a counselor in terms of his professional characteristics: He has intelligence, which involves a breadth "perception of relationships among events," the ability to "symbolize experience" and

to interpret life with "meaningful generalizations." The in-
telligent person is "articulate in communication." In the Hebrew sense of Proverbs, these are the characteristics of the
tebunah, the "man of understanding." He is skilled in "mo-
bilizing the resources of the environment and experience in
the services of a variety of goals." (Nelson N. Foote and
Leonard S. Cottrell, *Identity and Interpersonal Competence,*
p. 53; The University of Chicago Press, 1955.)

The pastoral counselor has empathy, which means that the
professional person can perceive situations from other people's standpoints. Thus he can anticipate and predict their
behavior. Pastoral counseling requires the capacity to "take
the role of the other," and "the absence of this is a sign of
misunderstanding" (*ibid.,* p. 54). He is autonomous, which
means that the professional person is capable of clarifying
his own conception of himself. He maintains independently
a "stable set of internal standards by which he acts." He is
"self-directed and self-controlled in his actions." He has "confidence in and reliance upon himself," and "maintains a
reasonable degree of self-respect"; he "has the capacity for
recognizing" that "real threats to self" can mobilize "realistic
defenses when so threatened." He has judgment, which means
"the ability to adjudicate among values, or to make correct
decisions; the index of lack of judgment (bad judgment) is
mistakes, but these are the products of an antecedent process
in which skill is the important variable" (*ibid.*). Referral,
consultation with other people than the counselee, even acceptance of responsibility for counseling in the first place,
all call for judgment.

The pastoral counselor demonstrates creativity, which
means that the professional person has "demonstrated the
capacity for innovations in behavior or real reconstruction or
any aspect of his environment." He has the ability to "develop fresh perspectives from which to view all accepted
routines and to make novel combinations of ideas and objects
and so define new goals, endowing old ones with fresh meaning and inventing means for their realization" (*ibid.,* pp. 55–

57). The pastoral counselor, particularly in the guidance of his counselees, is capable of inventing or improvising new roles or alternative lines of action in problematic situations and of inspiring such behavior in others. Many of his counselees are uncreative persons and continually find themselves in dilemmas and impasses. They are at their wits' end. They are shut up to a rigid adherence to one solution to their problems. A part of the professional competence of a pastoral counselor is to provide the creative kind of relationships in which innovations, inventions, and the discovery of new alternatives is a daily event. In short, this creativity engenders hope. When a counselee says, "There is nothing else I can do," often the very process of counseling itself is that "something else" which opens new avenues to hopeful existence.

A *third characteristic of the pastoral counselor as a professional person, as Seward Hiltner has said, is that he has the capacity to define and clarify his responsibilities in terms of basic principles and not just techniques or means.* This is the effort of this whole volume. Some emphasis has been given to pastoral counseling as technique, but much attention has been given to the development of the pastor's conception of himself and his understanding of the basic principles upon which his work as a counselor stands. Similarly, this applies to the relationship of a pastoral counselor to his counselee. He is not simply manipulating the person toward a chosen end of his own, but is working with the person in the development of basic principles for living. For example, the care of bereaved persons is based upon the principle of "working through" the various stages of grief. This is the principle; clinical technique grows out of it. Furthermore, marital conflict is a process of deterioration of trust, communication, and covenant. The technique of marriage counseling grows out of a detailed understanding of this process of deterioration and its arresting and reversal.

A *fourth characteristic of the pastoral counselor as a professional person rests in his equipment and training.* The Protestant Reformation and Vatican II have shifted the emphasis from the structure of the church to that of a person equipped and trained to do the work of ministry. The pastoral counselor depends upon neither his "personage" nor the institution of the church for his professional competence as a counselor. He must have submitted himself to the disciplines and training that equip him as a counselor. These disciplines include both the classical and the neotraditional types of training in the pastoral ministry. The pastoral counseling movement in America has rightly concentrated much attention and energy upon the development of professionally valid forms of clinical pastoral education for the minister. The processes of accreditation, qualification, and authorization of the pastor as a counselor are of great importance to Protestant theological educators.

Certification of Professional Ministers

Since 1961 at least three different organizations have set about training, certifying, and unifying ministers who have had specialized training as counselors, teachers of clinical pastoral education, and functioning parish ministers.

The American Association of Pastoral Counselors has been organized and now lists a membership of 715 in its categories of diplomate, fellow, members, etc. This organization, according to Howard Clinebell, has confronted the dangers of "losing its roots and context—i.e., that it will become estranged from the shepherding image of the pastor, from a religious view of existence, and from a responsible relationship with the community of faith which is the church" (Howard Clinebell, "Creative Interaction Between the Generalist and the Specialist in Pastoral Counseling," *The Pastoral Counselor*, Spring, 1964, pp. 3–12). At about the same time I questioned the issue of specialization and asked: "How do you . . . keep (pastoral counseling) from going the way of professional evangelism as a subprofession of the ministry?" Clinebell most recently has said that we have avoided the dangers he earlier named. I think that they are still there in greater force. I agree with James Glasse when he says: "The battle will

continue, but the issue is clear. If pastoral counseling develops
as an autonomous specialty, it must either become a separate
profession or must make clear how professional expertise in
the pastoral role is related to the ministerial profession."
(James D. Glasse, *Profession: Minister,* p. 66; Abingdon Press,
1968.)

Glasse himself has participated with Granger Westberg
and others in establishing the American Academy of Parish
Clergy with standards of certification based on specific
amounts of study in workshops, clinics, and seminars. Every
three years a member would be required to show evidence
of continuing education—not as a student, but as a prac-
ticing professional as over against being an amateur. My own
experience in considerable participation in such "colleague-
to-colleague" on-the-job training has been that these pastors
learn more rapidly, concretely, and operationally than they
did when they were students. One of the main deterrents
to learning among theological students is the perpetuation
of their delayed adolescence in the role of student per se.

A third professional organization of ministers is the Association for Clinical Pastoral Education. The main functions
of this organization are to provide clinical pastoral education
for theological students and active pastors, to see to it that
certified supervisors of high quality are doing the teaching,
and to accredit hospitals, schools, delinquency institutions,
churches, etc., as adequate centers for such education. In a
sense, this movement has provided some of the impetus for
the development of the sense of profession in the two previous organizations.

However, all three organizations have developed a model
of the equipment of the minister as a professional as opposed
to being amateur which has just now swept through theological schools in a subtle adoption of their premises in new
curricula for the Doctor of Ministry degree for ministers. The
ingredients of collegial, peer-group learning as over against
"over-under" teacher-student learning, of *supervised* on-the-
job field experience, of careful pastoral research (as distin-

guished from but not set over against literary-historical research) are in the designs of a considerable number of degree programs. This Doctor of Ministry degree can be a dream come true in raising the level of theological instruction to make genuine professionals and not just well-intentioned do-gooders of ministers. This can happen if adequate supervision is provided. The clinical pastoral education model has become too hidebound to the hospital setting. Clinical supervisors can inform the Doctor of Ministry programs if the clinical supervisors can and will be placed and can and will function in churches, denominational agencies, urban training centers, in slum storefronts, in the open marketplace, etc.

Yet the bureaucratic system of the Association for Clinical Pastoral Education has become a somewhat self-satisfied status system in its own right. The element of charisma flashes only occasionally. Anton Boisen once told me that the movement had hurried into "an early orthodoxy as to what supervision is and where it should happen." This has prevented creative experimentation, recognition of eccentric credit, and the development of a variegated and colorful array of individuality among supervisors. The next step in such a process is a reward of mediocrity for the one asset it contributes to a mass movement: conformity.

The Doctor of Ministry program offers a challenge to pastoral counselors and clinical supervisors to become involved with professors of the classical disciplines of the Biblical, historical, and ethical fields. On the other hand, these professors can become involved in the actual professional lives of students they instruct.

At the time of this writing, however, I have closely inspected the Doctor of Ministry degree program, based on consultations held by the American Association of Theological Schools, and on three years of curriculum committee work and teaching in the school where I teach. The publicity which advertises the degree calls it a *professional* doctorate. Yet the criteria of *what* a profession is, the disciplines of distinctly *pastoral* research, the logistics for retooling pro-

fessions for this kind of teaching, the nature of a distinctly
professional curriculum, and a clear pattern for equipping
field supervisors have been only dimly perceived as necessary;
still less have they been brought into being. The administra-
tions of seminaries seem to me to have panicked at declining
enrollments, decreased financial support, and bad public
relations. To them the Doctor of Ministry degree seems to be
an answer to the need for students, tuition, and denominational support. The necessity for additional faculty, the
training personnel resources required for academic supervision of pastors in the field, and the relief of already over-
loaded faculty personnel have been obdurately ignored. The
American Association of Theological Schools itself has yet to
provide leadership in these matters. They need funds to do
so.

Therefore, the professional education of ministers as a
dream may turn into a nightmare of inferior education, the
superimposition of false confidence in people who are called
"Doctor" but have not the foggiest concept of themselves
as functioning professionals, and theological education will
itself hurry its own demise.

I know that I am being severe in my utterances here. However, I am deeply committed to theological education as professional equipment for ministry. I am severe in my rejection
of any form of education that lacks serious substance. Men
would do well to consider my gloom about the Doctor of
Ministry as a deliberate attempt to aggravate excellence into
being when other valiant efforts have been ignored.

There are no good reasons for the state of the Doctor of
Ministry as I have assessed it. Good public relations could
be developed by initially selecting a group of pastors, church
executives, chaplains, campus ministers, etc., who seriously
want to learn how to teach as field supervisors. The first
group of Doctor of Ministry degrees should be given them
for undergoing a two-year program in the supervision of students; the students would thus receive Master of Divinity
credit for work done in the field under supervisors who them-

selves are being trained in supervision by an interdisciplinary team. Membership in this two-year program should be highly limited.

The second step would be the development of widely varied centers of training where several supervisors would regularly meet with their students as a group as well as meet with them weekly as individuals. "Campus 1980" should be redefined and cells of disciplined supervisors would come— not just from hospitals but also from campuses, churches, denominational and ecumenical headquarters, urban training centers, etc.

The third step would be to develop research projects that would bring historical, theological, and Biblical data into technical encounter with behavioral science methodology of validation and research. The field research project should be the apex and test of the candidate's total learning. Such projects *could* pool the resources of pastors, public school teachers, doctors, lawyers, business persons, and social agencies at the purist level.

This process should never be accomplished in less than two years. Such an approach would prevent the degree from being a retread of previous college or seminary work. The end objective would be a disciplined attack on the minister's concept that his work is something for which he was not educated and to replace this with an eye-to-eye relationship between him as a professional alongside other professionals in his community. It takes far more to make a professional person than a degree, a title, or a new piece of wallpaper for his office wall. It takes a laborer worthy of his hire because he can do with potency and competency what he is called to do.

My hope is that the American Association of Pastoral Counselors and the Association for Clinical Pastoral Education will not retreat into an ever-narrowing specialization that thrives on the middle classes only. My hope is that our members will use our skills in dealing with the deprived in institutions, to move pastors and parishioners to become involved in ministry to the downcast, the outcasts, the face-saving respectable, and the hard-nosed exploiters of the disadvantaged. The educational possibilities of the Doctor of Ministry degree are one avenue for developing a disciplined professional approach from within the churches.

However, if the American Association of Pastoral Counselors and the Association for Clinical Pastoral Education retreat into a narrower and narrower specialization of counseling and psychotherapy, we will move away from both the parish setting and the theological seminary. Then, as a separate profession, we will have to demonstrate to the Department of Health, Education and Welfare that we are indeed a viable health delivery profession. We will have to demonstrate to health insurance companies that we are authentic third-party recipients of benefits for having satisfied the health needs of people. We will have to convince companies in business and industry that we can contribute to workers' usefulness to the companies in lowering absenteeism, arresting and reversing alcohol and drug addiction, bringing greater marital harmony to workers, and increasing personnel morale. When we have accomplished this, we will be faced with the issue of our charisma—our gift of ministry as an unmerited favor of God, and our identity as ministers who are distinctly *pastoral* counselors. As a pastoral counselor, I am committed to the possibility and the ambiguity of the indispensability of both a sense of profession and a sense of charisma for each other. Yet to bring them on balance with each other calls for some discernment of the elusive meaning of charisma.

MEANINGS OF CHARISMA

Charisma is a special divine gift which is conferred by God upon a believer in God as evidence of divine grace. Charisma fits a person with a dynamic for his lifework, calling, or office. At its base, charisma is God's free gift of redemption, deliverance, and affirmation in the face of our sin, bondage, and self-rejection. Such deliverance calls for thanksgiving.

The life of suffering is met with the gift of grace. The gift of deliverance from suffering and bondage becomes the tool with which we participate in the deliverance of others. By means of the comfort with which we are comforted, we become a comfort to those with whom we counsel. (II Cor. 1:3–7.)

Distortions of Charisma

Yet this general meaning of charisma is distorted by well-meaning people both in Biblical times and in modern times.

Charisma as the Antithesis of Education. A considerable amount of anti-intellectualism is wrongly confused with charisma. The uneducated person may be suspicious of the person who is "fast with the words," likely to use his education to trap, overwhelm, or intimidate the uneducated person. The suspicions of the uneducated are not without some substance in reality, but their defense is often that the learned person lacks common sense, is stupid about the way life really is, and, as a religious person, does not "have the Spirit."

As one begins to edge toward the latter accusation—that the uneducated person lacks the Spirit—he begins to see the hidden assumption about charisma emerge: i.e., the uneducated are *given* wisdom, insight, ability to command the evil spirits that possess the lives of those to whom they minister. On this presupposition whole systems of folklore of the shaman, the Appalachian "granny," the Mexican-American *curandero,* and many others are built. The uneducated are often the poor and their struggle to survive is energized by the belief that the power to help, the wisdom to counsel, and the secrets of human suffering are gifts or charismata from God.

Charisma as a Particular Ritual. One of the most common distortions of charisma is to overidentify it with a particular ritual. For example, the "invitation" among churches of the revival tradition is the climax of the ceremony. The minister who preaches "stands or falls" in his own eyes and those of others as to how successful he is in getting people to make professions of faith. Such success is evidence of charisma, according to this distortion.

Another example is the experience of ecstasy in glossolalia. The person who "receives" this gift is actually named "charismatic." Sophisticated authors on cultism, such as E. T. Clarke, often use the word "charismatic" to mean ecstaticism and Pentecostalism.

Another example of a specific ritual being confused with charisma is the use of healing formulas. The mere performance of these rituals—anointing, laying on of hands, etc.—is often interpreted as charisma. It is possible to identify these rituals in and of themselves as charismatic, but to do so is a distortion.

The Grand Manipulator

The person who has the capacity to overwhelm and successfully to manipulate people in large numbers is often assumed to be charismatic. This person may have grown up in a chaotic environment in which he had to manipulate everyone and everything in order to survive. As he grew older, he became successful and no longer needed to manage, maneuver, and wheel and deal in order to survive. But by now he has come to enjoy manipulation for the sheer fun of being clever, exercising power, and overwhelming other people. Often this capacity is called charismatic when it would more accurately be called cleverness. Søren Kierkegaard drew the distinction best when he spoke of a person as having exchanged his call to be a prophet for his desire to be a genius.

Authentic Charisma

The Inherently Helpful Person. The genuinely charismatic person, in my opinion, is the therapeutic equivalent of Charles Truax's and Kevin Mitchell's valuable description of "the inherently helpful person." They say that such persons may have little, some, or much training. In all instances, regardless of training, however, the inherently helpful person possesses accurate empathy, nonpossessive warmth, and genuineness. These persons "have been rewarded for being helpful from their early formative years onward . . . these skills have been built upon and reflect fairly permanent personality characteristics." Truax and Mitchell say that if a person has these characteristics of accurate empathy, nonpossessive warmth, and genuineness, individuals who spend time with them "will be as helped, if not more helped, as if they were receiving formal counseling and psychotherapy from the socially sanctioned professional." (Charles B. Truax and Kevin M. Mitchell, "Research on Certain Therapist Interpersonal Skills in Relation to Process and Outcome," Allen E. Bergin and Sol L. Garfield, eds., *Handbook of Psychotherapy and Behavior Change*, p. 327; John Wiley & Sons, Inc., 1971.)

Cross-cultural Communication Capacity. The charismatic person—whether he is highly educated or not—has the capacity to move through the social class barriers that separate him from people. He can move among the aristocracy without feeling that he is owned by them or must be obeisant to them. He can move among unskilled laborers without communicating condescension. The Lord Jesus Christ was heard gladly by the common people and was unabashed by either the learned or the wealthy. In a sense, the charismatic person lives what Stephen Neill called "a genuinely human existence."

The characteristics of accurate empathy, nonpossessive warmth, and genuineness can be learned and improved with training. They improve cross-cultural communication capacity. They can be obscured and distorted when training forces an unauthentic mold upon a person, when status-anxiety short-circuits spontaneity, and when role-abrasion creates possessiveness in a power struggle over the person's approval who is being helped. As Glenn Asquith says, the pastoral counselor must be able to combine "technical knowledge with personal intuition in order to relate to others in a growth-facilitating manner" ("Professional Training and Charisma: Toward an Integration," p. 9; unpublished paper, 1973).

Charisma as the Power of an Existential Shift. We live in a world of blending and separating mythologies. We have scientific mythologies which are more sophisticatedly called "theoretical models" or "modalities." We also have older mythologies which are held firmly and sincerely by unlearned and unsophisticated people. Much wisdom resides in these older mythologies. They have a certain tenacity in the archetypal levels of being of even the most learned. In coping with scientific formulas, the pastoral counselor treats by rational guidance, insight release, and reordering the memories of persons with more constructive meaning. If he is a more aggressive, reality-oriented counselor, the pastor uses persuasion and habit-reconditioning. Only those pastors who are in touch with the deeper primitive aspects of human existence have the charisma to appeal to the older mythological and even magical depths of personality. Jan Ehrenwald provides an integrative approach to counseling and psychotherapy by making "proper allowance for myth and myth-induced shifts in the therapeutic process" (*Psychotherapy: Myth and Method,* p. vii; Grune & Stratton, Inc., 1966). The capacity to move with facility from one level of mythology—scientific and otherwise—honestly, with accurate empathy and nonmanipulative commitment to the well-being of "the other" is another way of describing charisma.

My hunch is that charisma is a gift from the point of view of one's relation to God. It is a certain raw courage to respond in a novel situation—which one has not experienced before and probably will never experience again—with a sense of divine imperative that what one is about to say or do is inherently helpful and unmistakably right. The Yiddish word *chutzpah* comes near it. One takes a plunge, says and does what the context, the moment, and the pain call for at the time. He unequivocally takes responsibility for his acts before God. When it is done, he marvels, thanks God, and is reluctant to tell anyone. Ordinarily, he "goes and tells no man."

An example of this sudden shift from a rational, reflective, and scientific frame of reference to a "plunge into persuasion" is found in the following critical incident of the ministry of a highly trained pastoral counselor.

Jane was a sixteen-year-old girl committed to a treatment center for juvenile delinquents after she repeatedly ran away from home. Soon after she entered the institution, Jane was referred to the chaplain by her social worker. The social worker explained that the girl had "not gotten over her mother's death." In conversation with Jane the chaplain learned that her mother had died six years before at a state mental hospital. At that time Jane learned that she had been adopted by an aunt and that the woman who died—whom she had thought to be her mother's sister—was, in fact, her mother.

Over a period of several weeks the chaplain came to know Jane as a girl who though basically healthy, according to a psychiatric evaluation, was experiencing a morbid grief reaction. In their conversations together the chaplain and Jane explored both her fantasies and the realities of her prolonged grieving. The basic dynamic was Jane's difficulty in forgiving and reaccepting her aunt as "mother" because she was plagued by a lingering feeling of being cheated of a relationship to her real mother. Jane's idea of her real mother was more fantasy than fact.

About two o'clock one morning the chaplain received a call at home with the request that he come and talk to Jane. The report was, "She says she sees her mother." The chaplain went to the cottage where Jane was a resident and found several security men with flashlights searching the area around the cottage. The chaplain asked about the situation and was told that one of the girls said that she saw somebody outside the cottage. The chaplain knocked on the cottage door. The cottage parent was hesitant to let the chaplain in because she was afraid the "spirit of Jane's mother might come in."

The chaplain said: "Open the door. The only spirit coming in with me is the Holy Spirit of God."

The chaplain asked the cottage parent to get the other girls to bed while he talked with Jane. Jane said that her mother was there standing outside by the streetlight. The chaplain talked with Jane about what her mother's appearence meant to her. Her feeling was that her mother was only causing trouble for her. She said, weeping, "I wish she would go away and never come back." The chaplain asked if she could tell her mother how she felt. Jane said she was afraid. The chaplain asked if she would like him to tell her mother to leave. She emphatically said that she would. The chaplain opened the window, faced the streetlight, and said in a loud voice: "You have come to cause trouble—not to help. We do not want you here. As God's messenger I command you—leave and do not return."

Jane reports that her mother left that night and has not returned. The chaplain continued to see Jane on a regular basis for the next two months. She was able to complete her grief work rather quickly after this event. Two years later, at this writing, Jane is doing quite well and has renewed her relationship to her adoptive mother.

These things happen to extensively trained and highly professional persons. They do not teach these things to others because the events are nonrepetitive and cannot be reproduced by "method" or "technique" apart from a ripe timing, a serendipitous context, and an amazing amount of suffering, demonstrated competence, and hard-earned confidence from those to whom one ministers. I can record here such an instance, one that affirms Ehrenwald's "existential shift" hypothesis and my description in this paragraph. It is an event in the life of a seasoned and well-trained pastoral counselor and chaplain of a delinquency treatment center. I learned about it indirectly and persuaded him to let me record it here.

Charisma as the Stewardship of Gratitude to God. My own clearest conviction as to the meaning of charisma is that charisma is the disciplined giving of the gifts received by us from

God to others who reach out to us and to whom we reach out. The psychoanalytically treated person who is released from bondage through treatment gives much of that same release to others as David Roberts did through his book *Psychotherapy and a Christian View of Man*. A person who has come from a shattered home, but who by God's free gift was held together and was brought to love abounding by a charismatic teacher, in turn becomes a steward of this "good gift" from God. Charisma is then the stewardship of gratitude—gratitude to God for the comfort with which he has comforted us. The depths of gratitude become the instruments of *charis* or grace by means of which we care, counsel, empathize with, express nonpossessive warmth toward, and come through to others as being genuine.

Consequently, when counseling becomes pastoral, all the professional know-how is illumined by the charisma of gratitude and integrated into the one person without disharmony. When effective results express themselves, the charismatic professional is quite reluctant to claim credit; he is more likely to thank God, take heart, and move on to another place and person of need. He does not have time for cleverness, only for gratitude for the charismata of God.

Chapter 6

THE TEMPORARY
AND THE DURABLE

Pastoral counseling is always characterized by balancing the tension between temporary, specialized, and therapeutic relationships, on the one hand, and lasting, general, and durable relationships on the other hand. For example, a twenty-seven-year-old woman on the first interview with a pastoral counselor said: "I have lived ever since I have been a Christian on the assumption that with only God's help and my efforts combined I could face life successfully. Now that has collapsed. God and I cannot live life alone. We both need other people." The counselor responded by saying: "So you came to see me, another person?" She replied: "Yes, but you can be the other person only a short time. I need to learn how to trust someone over the long pull of the years, be it man, woman, or child."

This counselee stated the issue clearly. The tension between the temporary therapeutic relationship and the durable nourishing relationship for life could not be stated more specifically than she stated it.

THE TENSION IN PSYCHOTHERAPY

Short-Term vs. Long-Term Therapy

Freudian psychoanalysis has traditionally been an open-ended, long-term kind of therapy. Its goal has been "the psychoanalysis of the total personality." In my own clinical contact I have seen persons who had been in psychoanalysis for as long as twenty years. In shorter, three- and four-year programs of psychoanalytic treatment, I have done pastoral work with persons who were in acute anxiety attacks about the termination of treatment.

One such person sought to turn the pastoral counseling relationship into an analytic hour and abruptly ended the relationship when I refused to accept the role of psychoanalyst. Having learned from this situation, I was more creative with a second person. I saw her twice a week for four weeks, once a week for the next three months, and then changed the location of our interviews from a psychiatric clinic to my seminary office. I saw her for three more months on a twice-a-month basis in a religious setting, all the while concentrating, with her cooperation, on her distinctly religious concerns. I kept the therapeutic orientation in a distinctly reality-based approach to present behavior and realistic steps she could take to change her life situation.

Then I told her that I wanted her cooperation in breaking the interview habit. I told her that I wanted to end the interviews but that I would not abandon her. I would call her by telephone for a brief conversation and she could feel free to call me if she felt the need to do so. She could also write me and I would answer her letter.

She took the challenge and would write me about once a week during the first year. Then the letters diminished in number and their contents changed into a more positive mode of thought. About once every three weeks she would call me. I called her about once a month. On her own initiative, she became actively involved in a church that provided a considerable amount of emotional support and great quantities of affirmation of her ability as a teacher. She has been free of anxiety attacks, has had no need to write letters or to call, and has used no medication in the last three months.

This person was referred to me by a psychiatrist who conscientiously felt that therapy should not become a way of life. The natural resources of the ministry and the church can provide longer-term resources of a lasting kind, he felt. The family physician was then turned to for ongoing medical attention rather than to prolong psychiatric treatment.

Otto Rank was one of the first analysts to challenge the open-ended approach to treatment in psychotherapy. In his books *Will Therapy* and *Truth and Reality* he recommended a technique which he called "end-setting." He would come to an agreement with the person as to *how long* he expected to be in treatment. The buildup of anxiety as the "end" drew nearer was used therapeutically to prompt the person to courageous decision. More recently, the transactional analysis strategy of making a contract with the person is a further refinement of the effort to come to terms with the reality that therapy is no adequate substitute for the natural nutriments of durable life relationship to friends, colleagues, relatives, and neighbors. The contract consists of coming to terms with the amount of time that is to be used. Time is then translated into money and a fee is agreed upon.

At this writing, the use of fees to stabilize a longer-term use of time has reached a level of acceptance unheard of even ten years ago. The fee structure anticipates the "need to bring gifts" that appears in counseling relationships that have no fees. The fee offsets feelings of guilt the person has for taking "so much time." Furthermore, the fee structure tends to define the relationship as one in which the question of the counselor's motives for "doing good" are answered: so that he can care for his family's economy, recoup some of his costs for an education, and/or not feel imposed upon in the use of time. One of the most helpful aspects of the fees is to mark the beginning, mid-phases, and end of the formal counseling. Another aspect of the fee is the justification of counseling a person not of one's congregation, student body, etc., yet a person who should be nonparasitic in his use of pastoral time.

However, the use of fees is not culturally woven into the image of the minister's personal counseling and confessional work. Would the minister prefer to be paid for services rendered or be tipped? I had some second thoughts about all this when working in a low-income family counseling center. I happened—quite by chance—to draw a wealthy man as a counselee. We moved through to the third interview, at which time he became quite angry with me. He expressed it by saying: "You must not be very competent. I pay my caddy at the golf club more than I pay you!"

Even with such messages as this, the minister's tradition is saturated with a heavy taboo on the discussion of money and its place in both temporary and durable pastoral relationships. As a result, one-way covenants are assumed: The minister commits his time on an unconditional and undefined basis and the person who uses his time makes no commitment at all. The one-way covenant increases the pastor's anxiety, shortens his patience, and quickens the time when hostility may make a more temporary relationship than a fee-taking contract would. Yet because of the need to keep a steady cash flow, any kind of therapist may extend a relationship beyond the time that is most realistic for the counselee's own well-being.

The Contract and Money

The use of fees implies legal responsibility for the outcome of the counseling. Should therefore a pastoral counselor carry malpractice insurance? It raises the issue of state and federal inspection and licensing of pastoral counselors. The use of fees causes third-party payment problems—something just now being faced. Third-party payment means payment for services by medical insurance companies, Medicare, etc. Then, too, are fees for service by a pastoral counselor tax deductible on federal and state income tax?

Questions such as the ones in the previous paragraph are open and being explored at this time. Tactics such as receiving money as "gifts" to a church or a school have been used. The counselor does not receive the money as fees, but is paid a salary by the church or the school that receives the money as gifts. Another tactic is that of double competency in which a pastor is a certified and/or licensed psychologist. A more strategic approach is that of the American Association of Pastoral Counselors, which has made efforts to achieve legal recognition of its members as "health delivery" agents.

Tradition tends to prompt automatic rather than rational behavior. Traditionally, ministers have recoiled from fee-taking. Yet we have also been occasionally pampered, often paternalized, and more often rejected because of gifts, handouts, and minister's discounts.

Like a cast for a broken leg, a formal therapeutic relationship aims to set the life in the most authentic and satisfying direction and to hold the person steady in that direction until the great decisions of vocation, marriage, parenthood, trust in friend and in God are strong enough to justify removing the cast. The same analogy has been used by responsible psychiatrists today to describe the use of tranquilizers, mood elevators, and other such drugs. The "cast" is temporary.

Reality vs. "Sickness"

Reality therapy is the most recent form of psychological and psychiatric treatment that has challenged the antrogenic ill effects of long-term analysis of one's past. The concept of mental illness is laid aside in behalf of a concept of irresponsible and unethical behavior instead. Whereas I consider a meaningful acquaintance with the person's historical life story and life-style still an important part of formal pastoral counseling, I can resonate with William Glasser's emphasis upon the way in which the past can be used to avoid obvious responsibility in the present. Such approaches have served to focus the precise, expensive, and limited-in-time nature of the temporary therapeutic relationship. Yet, with the exception of Otto Rank, very few of these short-term therapists have dealt with the nature of the longer-term, natural relationships that sustain a person after therapy is over. Preventive psychiatrists such as Gerald Caplan emphasize how psychosocial supplies in the right quantity—not too little nor too much—can serve both to prevent mental breakdowns and to rehabilitate convalescents after therapy. Thereby they prevent relapses. A close look at traditional forms of pastoral care and neotraditional forms of pastoral counseling will reveal how the double responsibility of the past or for both short-term, temporary, therapeutic relationships and long-term durable relationships can be more true to life as it has to be lived.

PASTORAL COUNSELING
AMONG THE VARIED FORMS OF PASTORAL RELATIONSHIPS

The pastor's work as a counselor happens in the dynamic arena of his involvement with his counselees as neighbor and brother man in both the informal and formal relationships of the pastoral community. The pastor has a certain role in his counselee's life that may or may not be definite when that person, in the exigency of a moment, calls upon him for counseling help. This role is undefined in the confused and anxious mind of his counselee. The pastoral counselor must develop a great deal of canniness in clearly understanding himself and in communicating simply to the counselee the exact nature of his responsibilities as a pastor at any given moment. Whereas this responsibility for clarification rests upon all counselors, it rests more distinctly upon the shoulders of the pastoral counselor than any other. For example, the pastoral counselor does not have the kind of control either institutionally or professionally over his relationships as do other counselors, such as doctors. The doctor has a definite schedule: the patient always takes the initiative toward him; he can accept or reject the patient as one whom he is qualified to treat; or, he may terminate a relationship to a given patient through referral or discharge. This quite clearly defines his role, as compared with the work of the minister.

Therefore, the pastor must be alert and capable of understanding the difference between a confused interpersonal relationship, an informal relationship, and a formal relationship, and/or a combined formal and informal relationship. His approach, technique, and resources in dealing with persons in these varied kinds of relationships will be radically different.

Clarifying the Pastoral Counseling Relationship

The confused or unclarified relationship is one in which a pastor is seeking to discharge his formal responsibility as a pastor, and particularly as a pastoral counselor, in an informal, uncontrolled, undefined, unclarified situation. Usually this is because he does not understand the difference between a formal and an informal relationship. It may be because he rejects the more formal aspects of being a pastor. Or it may be due simply to neglect. He fails to clarify his relationship in conversation with his parishioner, ordinarily assuming that the relationship is clear. As a result he may attempt to communicate with his counselee through the overcast of confusion covering the relationship.

Confusion happens in several ways. First, *the time factor* may be out of control. The person presents a problem under the hurried circumstance of the moments just before a morning service is to begin. The pastor hurriedly attempts to deal with a major difficulty that simply cannot be dealt with in a short preoccupied moment of divided attention. This confuses both him and the counselee. He would have done better to have given brief support, affection, and encouragement and to have rescheduled a later time in which the whole matter could be dealt with more leisurely.

Secondly, *the place factor* may be out of kilter. The pastor may be standing on the corner of the main street of the city. He does not have the privacy that is needed, nor does he have the undivided attention that is required. He schedules the conference for a later time when he can see the person in the privacy of his counseling room. The privilege of a visit to the pastor's home or study to confer privately about a serious problem is in itself a form of encouragement, and at the same time brings clarity and control into the relationship.

A third way of clarifying a relationship is to be sure that *the degree of initiative and of responsibility* are fairly evenly balanced. One of the hallmarks of the pastoral ministry is that we have the right to take initiative toward people, to go to them, and to express concern about them.

However, we respect the privacy and the individual freedom of a person in the process of taking initiative. Our objective should be to stimulate their own initiative in such a way that they will want help with whatever degree of initiative we take toward them. In other words, we are confusing our relationship to people when we take full responsibility for all the initiative. We relieve them of the health and strength that comes to them when they are stimulated to be wholesomely concerned about their own destinies. The more typical example of this is when a person asks us to go to see a third person. The relationship is likely to become inflamed and confused if some form of welcome on the part of the third person is not sought. Likewise, it would make for a clearer relationship if the person who requests that the pastor visit the third person would suggest to that person that he come to the pastor or, at best, ask him if he would mind if the pastor visited him. A part of the great skill of being an effective pastor is in knowing where the line of balance for the initiative between the counselor and the counselee lies. This problem has been dealt with at length in books such as Professor Hiltner's volume on pastoral counseling and in the *Introduction to Pastoral Counseling* under the editorship of this author. The confused relationships of pastoral counselors often are to be attributed to a lack of clarification of the problem of initiative.

The fourth factor in confused relationships that needs clarification is *the particular identity in which the minister himself is functioning*. The minister is caught up as family member and as neighbor and as personal friend and brother man in relation to those whom he serves as pastoral counselor. He has anonymous relationships, such as contacts on buses, trains, planes, and in the open community. He has diffuse social relationships in the marketplace contacts, the recreational and social functions of the community, and the host-guest relationships of his own home. He has personal-friend relationships by reason of the fact that the church is a durable fellowship. A repetitive series of counseling interviews is only a small part of a good pastoral relationship. These people are his friends. He has family relationships to his wife, to his children, to his own siblings, and to his mother and father, as well as to the in-laws and more distant relatives. All these informal relationships are woven into the web of his formal functions as a minister and can be very easily confused with them.

Therefore, a pastor needs to know when and when not to activate the more formal dimensions of his task as a minister, particularly at the point of structuring or defining a counseling relationship. When he does this well he demonstrates skill in clarifying, both in his own mind and in that of his parishioner, the exact character of their relationship. They may jointly choose that the minister be related in an informal, supportive way as a friend; they may explicitly agree that the more distinctly social aspects of their relationship be kept to a minimum while the more serious work of counseling is in process. This is usually done in an exploratory interview in which a plan is made. A covenant based on trust and mutual understanding is carefully defined. This evaluative interview is a necessary prelude to any long-term counseling relationship. A spirit of reciprocity and rapport must be developed between the pastor and the counselee if any clear-cut progress is genuinely to be made in further counseling interviews. The pastor himself may, on the basis of a mutual sense of clarity between him and his counselee, decide that a longer-term series of counseling conferences between them is indicated. On the other hand, the pastor may define his role less formally and request referral of the counselee to another counselor (either a pas-

toral counselor or another kind of professional) who will perform the more detailed and formal functions. Such a counselor
may be more socially unrelated to the person and thus able
to offer more privacy. He may be in a fee-taking relationship
and thereby able to give more time on a less guilt-producing
basis. He may be less involved in the ongoing life of the counselee and in such a role that he can terminate the relationship
at an appropriate time.

The informal relationships tend to have great durability,
lasting over several decades, even. The formal relationships
of precisely graduated amounts of time are more temporary
and less durable. An exact discussion of the time element in
the therapeutic situation of formal counseling makes this
much clearer.

The Time Element in Pastoral Counseling

An increasingly larger group of parish pastors, hospital
chaplains, and full-time pastoral counselors are doing formal,
longer-term counseling and psychotherapy. Many of them
have had extensive and depth training in how to perform this
ministry. The time element is an extremely important factor.

Such pastors develop a disciplined use of time in multiple-
interview encounters. The pastor encourages the person,
through the processes of spiritual maturity and insight, to lay
hold of and to deal with his own problem. But he is not left
alone. The pastor gives him spiritual fellowship and assistance
in the pilgrimage of growth. He is not alone. For a time,
counseling pastors assumed that if they simply listened to a
person, this in itself was what was needed and all that was
needed. More recently, pastors are discovering that their willingness to listen to people's troubles in and of itself is a
symbolic way of saying things to the person that words cannot.
A nonverbal kind of communication is going on. The symbolic
act of scheduling a second interview, for instance, may say to
the person many different things: "I am not too busy to take
your problem seriously." Or it may say, "I think your problem

is serious." Or it may say, "I know you came for my 'answer,'
but I am treading water until I can think of one." These are
just a few of the things that scheduling a second interview can
mean to the person.

On the other hand, the pastor may hit resistance in the
scheduling of a second interview. The person may be an extremely demanding and passively dependent individual. He
insists that if he is the kind of pastor he ought to be, he could
just settle the whole matter right there. A passive-aggressive
person may forget to show up for the second appointment. An
openly hostile person may simply tell the pastor off for suggest-
ing that he needs help. In other words, a more intensive pastoral counseling is not just a matter of listening to people,
although this is a very great and important part of it. The nonverbal communication going on within the context of the total
relationship is in itself a healing light or a threatening irrita-
tion, or both. The pastor has to listen to this with what
Theodor Reik has called "the third ear."

The pastor must clearly define a mutually acceptable and
mutually understood counseling relationship for what it really
is. What is it? It is a process relationship of several interviews
in which the pastor and the parishioner explore together the
deeper ramifications and the larger and longer purposes of the
parishioner's life itself. This becomes an existential encounter
once it is established. A process of precounseling, however,
must precede it on the uncontrolled and undefined and often
confused relationships of the pastoral situation. Too much so-
called nondirectiveness on the part of the pastor in the construction of a defined counseling relationship can actually
break the contract the parishioner finds meaningless.

Precounseling usually happens in the first interview. The
pastor is still faced with the responsibility of knowing how to
make the best use of *one hour* in pastoral interviewing. Unlike
many social workers, psychologists, and psychiatrists, the pastor has to do his own "intake interviewing." The first interview
tends to be exploratory. Usually a third or more of the time in
a first interview is required to "hear the person out" as much

as that amount of time will permit. Several questions need to be asked on a first interview: (1) How long has the trouble been upon the individual; when did it start? (2) What attempts have been made to solve the difficulty, and especially to whom else has the counselee been for help? (3) How did the person decide to seek out the pastor? (4) What are the various alternatives of which the person has thought as possible solutions? If, in the process of the first interview, one sees that a longer-term relationship is indicated, he may suggest this as one additional alternative and frankly explain what the process of counseling has to offer as well as what its limitations are. If the person sees and accepts the validity and wisdom of this procedure, then a second interview is more easily scheduled.

In both instances—that in which one interview is used and that in which a multiple-process relationship is initiated for pastoral counseling—the use of time symbolizes the pastor's concern and his understanding of the person. To a great extent also the establishment of such a relationship is a shared appraisal of seriousness. The relationship tends to be made or broken in the first interview. The pastor's firmness and gentleness in interpreting his limitations and his resources to help the person make the difference. A careful management of the time relationship, then, is one mode of communicating understanding of the counselee.

Certain technical problems are involved in the use of time in pastoral counseling. For instance, one of the first questions asked is about *the length of an interview*. An interview kept within the scope of an hour tends to be most effective. The pastor may shorten it for the person who is unaccustomed to formal office situations, such as young children, relatively uneducated persons, and persons in much physical pain. He may lengthen the interview for the person who has traveled a long distance or has some other great handicap in coming for a conference. *The number of interviews* varies in terms of the basic need of the person. However, as we shall see later, the social and structural limitations of the pastoral relationship prevent him from spending any great number of interviews with any one person. It may be that we shall sooner or later define pastoral counseling in terms of the five-to-ten interview situation in which we deal with more or less specific problem areas of the individual's life, such as bereavement, vocational choice, marital choice, and the making of a basic religious decision as to one's relationship to Christ.

However, pastors have become increasingly more active and competent to manage deeper, longer-term, and more formal types of relationships. The more time one uses in any given relationship the more important it becomes that he shall have had intensive and extensive clinical pastoral education under careful and mature supervision. When pastors accept such responsibility, they obligate themselves for training commensurate with the responsibility they accept. Even a full year of clinical pastoral counseling education in and of itself is not sufficient. But when a pastor has intensive psychotherapeutic training, he soon goes beyond the kinds of ecclesiastical support he can ordinarily secure. The complicated issues involved in the support of formal counseling have already been discussed in previous chapters.

Time and the Changing Meanings of the Pastoral Situation

The technical problems involved in the pastoral use of time in counseling raise some deeper issues as to *the quality and meaning* of the relationship of pastoral counseling. This changes at different phases of pastoral counseling in terms of the time encounter. A pastor's relationship, in one respect at least, derives some of its meaning, direction, and purpose from the amount of time that he is able to use with a given individual. A rough guide is somewhat as follows:

One Interview. A pastor has to be more time conscious and more directive. In a one-interview situation he depends more upon the shortcuts that his experience has taught him. He gives information; he gives support; he points out other resource people upon whom the counselee may call; he may guardedly answer questions quite directly; he may even give opinions. He gives these in an atmosphere of tentativeness. He carefully leaves the relationship "open" in the event that the person wants to come back to him. Too often pastors have confused openness and honesty with people (who are in as full a possession of their powers for living as he is) with "directiveness" in counseling. The actual fact of the matter is that the pastor does not have a counseling relationship in a one-interview situation if the way we have technically defined it here is correct.

Two to Six Interviews. Here the pastor is usually involved in short-term crisis or situational counseling. It is largely supportive and reflective, and intensely pastoral in nature. The immediate depths to which second- and third-interview relationships can go are amazing, especially when the counselee has been in classes that the pastor has taught or in worship services that he has conducted. The pastoral role is more significant in some areas of the country and in black communities than in others. It strikes the deeper and more unconscious mechanisms of the personality more quickly and more certainly within certain cultures than it does in others. The pastor in a clearly defined religious culture quite often finds a depth dimension in his relationship to a counselee on the second or third interview. A professional psychotherapist would need several more interviews in which to elicit such response. One of the unexplored areas of research for pastoral counseling is the qualitative difference it shows when done by black pastors with black counselees.

Seven to Ten Interviews. The quality of relationship here varies also in terms of the clarity of the role of the counselor. However, if a relationship sustains this long, one is justified in saying that the pastor is involved in a more intensive kind of pastoral counseling. Deeper dynamics and mechanisms of identification, projection, transference, etc., tend to become active. The more aggressive and authoritarian the pastor is, the more likely these are to be set in motion. Likewise, the social situation of the pastor begins to strain. The counselee is likely to want to involve him in social relationships. He gets invitations to dinner, requests for a visit at his home, ministries to members of his family who may be sick, etc.

The basic limitations of the ordinary pastoral relationship for a more or less professional psychotherapeutic endeavor begin to emerge. The social role of the pastor's wife is also brought into play. (This is one unique factor in the Protestant minister's task: he is usually married and his wife knows and is called upon to respond to his counselees, both men and women.) Likewise, the community as a whole begins to ask tacitly: "What is the meaning of all of this going and coming?" The pastor may assure the counselee of confidential treatment of all that he says to him. On the other hand, the pastor himself has no assurance of the same kind of confidential treatment from the counselee. The counselee may talk rather vividly and avidly of what goes on in the interview sessions. This in itself must be handled both strategically and tactically in such a way as to contribute to, rather than detract from, the pastor's other functions.

Eleven and/or More Interviews. If the pastor has been faithful and effective up to this point in counseling, he begins to see more unconscious psychological material emerging in the counseling conferences. The counselee may begin to deal with dream material, to involve members of his own family in the drama, to make referrals to the pastor of other people with whom he is related, and to become almost a member of the pastor's family if he has been permitted to involve the pastor socially in the earlier stages of the relationship. If he decides to end the relationship, the pastor has a very definite problem as to what sort of durable relatedness he can offer the counselee in the normal interactions of community living.

The Time Factor and the Pastoral Use of Community Resources

Obviously, the above rough guide of the shifting meaning of the pastoral counseling relationship in terms of the time factor suggests that the pastor has more than one reason for asking for the help of other community resource persons for more professional types of counseling. Therefore, the time factor in pastoral counseling becomes a very real issue as an indication for referral. A referral system is indispensable for any effective, formal pastoral counseling. One of the reasons that pastors do not have time to do their pastoral ministry is that they insist on doing it all themselves. They do not evaluate the resources of their church and community for giving assistance to individuals. They have failed to build a detailed knowledge of their community as to the agencies, professional and private practitioners, etc., who could help them in their task. Occasionally pastors call long distance by telephone to ask their former teachers in pastoral care to see one of their parishioners. Occasionally the professor can suggest someone in their own home city about whom they did not know. In one instance, the person to whom I referred the pastor was only a few doors down the street from him!

The amount of time that most pastors can legitimately give to one individual begins to be strained when they go beyond the tenth interview. Pastors often use more interview time than this, sometimes wisely and sometimes not so wisely. However, when they do so, they defy their own limitations in dealing with a person's problems. They are likely to create undue guilt problems in their counselee, particularly if he is a more depressed kind of person. Such a person has to be reassured again and again that the pastor has the time that he really does not have! If the counselee is a passive, dependent individual, the pastor creates hostility problems for himself in that the counselee may use the time poorly and lean dependently on the pastor as a crutch. The counselee, in many instances, will feel the need to give the pastor something. He brings him gifts, offers services, and may even seek to pay for the "services." These actions are highly symbolic and may obligate the pastor in strange and embarrassing ways. On the other hand, their symbolism may often involve forms of worship of God to which the pastor is only incidental. Therefore, we know that when a pastor goes beyond the tenth or eleventh interview with a person he is moving out of a distinctly simple pastoral context and into a highly complex type of relationship. Great sensitivity and responsible maturity are imperative.

Some Theological Dimensions of the Temporary and the Durable in Pastoral Counseling

The depths of the time factor in pastoral counseling reach the eternal issues of man's destiny. The pastoral necessity of doing more formal types of counseling raises some fundamental theological and ecclesiastical problems. What is the purpose of the church and its ministry? What is this pastoral relationship like, essentially?

Can a pastor "break" his relationship with a counselee, or is it, by its intrinsic character, a durable, eternal relationship? The pastor does not "discharge" his counselees. Instead, in terms of his purposive relationship to the church, he hopes that they will become members of the lasting fellowship of the Christian community. Consequently, he more than any other counselor shifts back and forth from one level of communication to another. At best, eventualities do occur. Several observers have noted how in a few instances a pastor does a very effective job of pastoral counseling and in the process of it loses rather than gains a new member. He may join someone else's church! On the other hand, at certain stages of pastoral counseling, the counselee may join his church as a demonstration of appreciation to him. This makes it necessary that the pastor have a "synoptic" view of his theology and church polity in relation to his pastoral counseling practice. His doctrine may become a whetstone upon which the spiritual understanding of his counselee is sharpened. His counselee may cause him to reexamine his doctrine.

Furthermore, the persistent tendency of counselees to involve the family life of the pastor indicates something definite about the intrinsic nature of the minister's being as a family man. At the same time, this presents a real conflict when the pastor begins to perceive himself in an identity similar to that of the psychologist, psychiatrist, etc. These kinds of counselors are "private" in a way that the pastor is not. Conflict can occur in terms of the traditional role of the pastor as a visitor in the home when it conflicts with the newer concept of pastoral counseling in which the person is expected by the pastor to come to see him in his study.

In such involvements, the anxiety of the pastor mounts. If he cannot bring this relationship with a counselee to a clear closure, what is the inherent meaning of his continuing encounter with the counselee? In addition to all that has been mentioned, the counselee transfers deep feelings of love and hate to him. He in turn develops an array of feelings about the counselee. For instance, pastors quite anxiously discuss in great detail the times that members of the opposite sex, and sometimes members of the same sex, interpret their relationship to them as a more distinctly erotic or sexual relationship. One rarely hears a pastor discuss quite so freely his own erotic feelings. These feelings he carries in the private soliloquy of his soul at worst, and at best in the I-Thou encounter he has with God in prayer. His anxiety over these feelings may cause him to retreat from a relationship. He may break a relationship at its most crucial point and just at the time when he was on the verge of breaking out of his role as pastor, counselor, etc., and into his role as a fellow human being, a fellow sinner, a fellow child of God, one whose limitations his counselee accepts and affirms even as he has learned to accept and affirm the counselee's limitations. On the other hand, he may continue a counseling relationship past a time of redefinition because it meets his own needs.

As has already been noted, Otto Rank says that within the therapeutic relationship there is an end-setting which may be used either redemptively or destructively. In his therapy, he agreed upon the limitations of time that both he and the counselee were suffering and jointly set an end to their relationship in its formal aspects. He likened this end to a death-birth in which an old restricted self died and a new and more potential self was born. The pastor does not have to set ends in his relationships quite so rigidly. Natural life has itself set ends in the great crises of human existence: birth, choice of a vocation, illness, old age, death—these are ends that are set within the habitation of man.

The time factor in pastoral counseling has its deepest relevance when the pastor realizes the tremendous sense of the eschatological dimension of life with which even the untutored tend to live in the face of these great crises. The processes of judgment are wrought out here. The *quo vadis?* is asked. What is the end of this relationship, this era in life, to mean in terms of the whole of life? The recent reemphasis upon man's hope in the midst of time-binding sets pastoral counseling in the context of a theology of hope. God has set the bounds of our habitation, and the binding of time thrusts us into the ultimate concerns of our existence. As the Moffatt translation of Deut. 29:29 puts it, "The hidden issues of the future are with the Eternal our God, but the unfolded issues of the day are with us and our children for all time, that we may obey all the orders of this law."

No matter how much of a pastor's time a given person shall require, that person necessarily shall have reached a certain level of despair before he seeks pastoral counseling. Many times his personal defenses against the stresses of life are largely shattered. He lives from day to day in the nameless intuition "that years of life can be pressed out of him," by the catastrophes and prolonged duresses under which he lives. He senses that time has run out or is about to run out. Harold G. Wolff cites abundant clinical evidence in which such persons simply "stare out into space and die" for the lack of hope. Wolff calls it give-up-itis, with which, in spite of our pseudo sophistication, large numbers of those both in and out of the church suffer. The task of the pastoral counselor is so to mobilize the resources of time that eternity may break through to proclaim a "hope that does not disappoint" to those who sit in regions of despair. For, as Wolff again says, "man is capable of enduring incredible burdens and taking cruel punishment when he has self-esteem, hope, purpose, and belief in his fellows" (Harold G. Wolff, M.D., "What Hope Does for Man," *Saturday Review*, 40:42–45, January 5, 1957).

Regardless of how much or how little time the pastor has with a given person under stress, his unique identity as a man of hope, as a son of encouragement, should remain constant. This ministry of hope is the meeting place of time and eternity in the good news of Jesus Christ.

Chapter 7

AGGRESSIVENESS VS. PASSIVITY

Since the beginning of the modern counseling movement among pastors, the issue between being aggressive or being passive in relation to persons has been a moving line of scrimmage in both the training and the practice of pastoral counselors.

THE DILEMMA

Various patterns of action and reaction in pastoral counseling have produced different modes of theory and practice.

Priest or Evangelist? Counselor or Preacher?

The issue of aggressiveness or passivity surfaces in such statements as "You can't help someone unless he asks for help." "You should listen to people and not interrupt what they are saying." The issue also surfaces in pastors' questions: "How can I get someone who has not asked for help to come to me?" The issue of aggressiveness or passivity is complicated in its ambiguity by the historical images of the pastor as a priest and as an evangelist. Stereotypes of the priest portray confession as a ritual in which the penitent *comes to* the priest. Similar stereotypes of the evangelist portray the minister as always taking the initiative, going to people, confronting them with their need for salvation. The pastor is made to feel guilty if he is not this aggressive. Furthermore, the pastor's task as a preacher is often equated with being aggressive toward people; it is often thought of as antithetical to his work as counselor, the latter being considered an inherently passive ministry. Also, as an ethicist representing the moral codes of the religious community, the pastor is seen stereotypically as being aggressive toward or over against other people. All these stereotypes are *partially* true, but they oversimplify the confessional ministry, the work of evangelism, the nature of preaching, and the ways of communicating ethical values. Other paradoxical elements go into all of these. Yet when the pastor affirms the more passive and dialogical elements in these ministries without denying the aggressive elements, he accepts the tension that goes with the ambiguity.

Doctor or Pastor? Nondirective or Confrontational?

Another instance of the dilemma between passive and aggressive elements is presented in the medical model for pastoral counseling and the more nondirective and client-centered methods of counseling and psychotherapy. The medical profession has a long history of ethical taboo against moving toward people aggressively to "get patients." The physician waits until the patient seeks help. If the patient leaves his care "against medical advice," the physician does not "go after" him to get him to return. The fact that much—though not all —clinical pastoral education has taken place in hospitals has caused many pastoral counselors trained there to assume by association much of the same stance toward people. Yet, as I shall seek to demonstrate, the pastor can learn from the medical model without being entrapped by it. He has other cultural options within his heritage and he can take the initiative toward people. In fact, his identity as a pastor involves the hope on the part of many people that he will move toward them, and their disappointment when he does not do so.

Furthermore, within the discipline of pastoral counseling,

early emphases upon listening and later emphases upon nondirective methodology in counseling have habituated several
seminary generations of pastoral counselors to a passive approach to counseling. To be aggressive, to interpret, to be
verbal, or to lead or guide were "non-okay" responses. To persuade, to command, or to forbid were distinctly "wrong" and
even unethical in the method of instruction received by many
pastors as pastoral counselors. In somewhat compulsive reaction against this, more recent emphases on reality therapy
have swung to the opposite extreme of heavy confrontation
with little or no common sense, much less empathy. In either
instance, the tension of the inseparableness of the aggressive
and the passive elements in human life is avoided. The result
is a sort of "one-sided" neurotic view of a part of life, after the
Jungian view of neurosis. Neither Carl Rogers, the main
exponent of client-centered therapy, nor William Glasser, the
main and best exponent of reality therapy, would assent to
such "one-sided" uses of their approaches to treatment. Inter-
preters who simplify their approaches into a "method-actor"
kind of counseling do seem to me to arrive at quick closure
on a one-sided kind of passivity or aggressiveness. The end
result is an inauthentic existence in either event. In other
words, the counselor is not an open self who is, as Aristotle
said, "just who he is and nothing else."

Pastoral Work or Pastoral Counseling?

An even further explication of the dilemma between the
aggressive and the passive dimensions of life is the tension between the pastoral work a minister does within his parish and
the individual, formal counseling he does in his office or study.
The pastor meets people in informal social settings, in the
marketplace of the community, in after-meeting conversations,
in the activities of agencies other than the church such as the
public school, the political structures, etc. The pastor does
much of his caring for people through media of communication other than the formal office visit or group counseling session. For example, he uses the letter, the telephone call, and

the pastoral visit to the business, the home, the hospital. He uses the professionally ritualized process of the breakfast, luncheon, coffee break, or dinner as a medium for relating deeply to people as he both gives and receives hospitality.

These media for the communication of concern and help represent a wide spectrum of degrees or intensities of aggressiveness and passivity. They are profoundly related to but not equatable with the precise instrument of the formal counseling interview and/or counseling session. The formal counseling relationship—whether individual or group—is woven into the social fabric of the larger social interactions of the parish minister, priest, or rabbi. The degree of aggressiveness or of passiveness fluctuates as both limitation and opportunity for the parish clergyman. Ordinarily his perception of these fluctuations is automatic and intuitive. It can be improved with conscious use of these fluctuations of relationships as "tools" rather than as pesky limitations to be endured, avoided, denied, or ignored. Russell Dicks at the outset of his work with pastors called the situations in which the pastor functioned outside the consultation room "pastoral work" and those in the consultation room "pastoral counseling." (By this he did not mean to infer that one was "work" and the other was "play"!) In Chapter 6 of this book, I have called the one pastoral relationship "informal" and the other "formal." Initiative, that amalgam of aggressiveness and passivity, was identified as one factor in the necessary clarification of the pastor's relationship.

However one names these changing intensities of aggressiveness and passivity, the pastor is not long at his work before he begins to see that the formal counseling interview—individual or group—is only a part of his significant, wisdom-imparting-and-receiving relationships to people. He then begins to search for a larger concept and strategy. If he finds one, what he has learned in his training about pastoral counseling is enriched, enlarged, and deepened. If he does not find a comprehensive strategy, he may reject his training in pastoral counseling as "very nice" but "inapplicable" to the parish.

The central objective of this chapter is to suggest such a strategy by devising a balancing principle for the tension between being aggressive and being passive as a pastoral counselor in the context of the parish, the school, or the hospital.

INITIATIVE: THE BALANCE BETWEEN AGGRESSIVENESS AND PASSIVITY IN COUNSELING

For purposes of discussion and clarity I suggest that *initiative* is a "least common denominator" between aggressiveness and passivity. The pastor's aggressiveness or passivity arises from his *being*. He may *be* an aggressive person, and it will take all sorts of effort or initiative to remain silent, to do nothing, to wait. He may *be* a passive person, and a small measure of initiative or effort on his part will "come through" to his counselee as more dramatic than much more initiative on the part of an aggressive person. A least common denominator such as initiative (i.e., effort) can be measured and calibrated by the kind of tool that fits the relationship, the time, and the seriousness of the problem facing a counselee. Therefore, two observations about initiative can be made here.

"Minus" Factors in Initiative

First, initiative has a plus and a minus dimension in aggression and in passivity respectively. The massive discipline required of an aggressive pastoral counselor to listen, to *allow* the processes of growth to happen, to trust the counselee to make his own decisions, calls for much effort. The minus factor of initiative is expressed in the following clinical encounter of a member of a seminar of the Stone Foundation Project on Pastoral Initiative which I conducted. Participants kept a journal of their work. We shall draw upon the journal of one participant for the following account.

In an October 1, 1970, entry in his journal John Boyer says: "Today I went to Norton to meet with Dr. Hayes and the patient to whom he was to assign me. Dr. Hayes first talked with

Mr. M., explaining what he wanted to do by way of bringing me into the treatment program for Mr. M. I was then introduced to Mr. M. after he had expressed the desire to think over whether or not he wanted to enter into an additional relationship with another person, namely, me. I told Mr. M. about myself to try to give him something to go on in deciding about this. After five minutes Dr. Hayes terminated our interview and asked me to wait for him until he finished with Mr. M. Later he talked with me, saying that Mr. M. would call me if he wanted me. Otherwise I was to make no move at all toward Mr. M. Dr. Hayes told me to report any contact with Mr. M. and to be back on October 15 when Mr. M. had his next appointment with him, Dr. Hayes. He wants me there in case Mr. M. wants to see me. Dr. Hayes said that Mr. M. needs all the support and encouragement he can get. Dr. Hayes told me he would assign me to another patient if Mr. M. did not want to activate his relationship with me. . . . I was a little disappointed at not getting on the way with Mr. M., but it is a delicate situation. This is one of those times when one must do nothing but wait. I suppose one could also pray. So I will."

The end result of this situation was that Mr. M. never did contact John Boyer.

At the November 19, 1970, meeting of the seminar the whole group met with Dr. Ray Hayes. As Mr. Boyer recorded it, the focus of the conversation turned to his (Mr. Boyer's) frustration because he had made no contact at all with the patient assigned to him. Dr. Hayes said that Mr. Boyer should be highly rewarded for his remarkable self-control and patience. Dr. Hayes pointed out that a sociocultural factor in the developmental history of the patient had stymied the development of a relationship. The man comes from an upper-class family and would not reach out for a distinctly pastoral kind of help. Dr. Hayes continued: "Sometimes an inability to do anything at all, to follow through in any way, may mean the most significant job of all. Mr. Boyer brings out data not brought out anywhere else in this seminar. Just standing and waiting is a contribution. Paradoxically enough, *not* being aggressive may be a form of initiative. The patient with whom Mr. Boyer was working is a man who wants to live on a guaranteed income without effort. The pastor and other professional people must add, to the three dimensions of a room, the dimensions of time and motion." Dr. Hayes said further that Boyer's success in this particular instance is defined in terms of getting negative results. Thinking in negative numbers was a breakthrough in the field of mathematics. Algebra is built on that. Negative factors are necessary for correcting misimpressions of positive results. By not doing anything at all, Boyer got results.

According to Mr. Boyer's account of the seminar, Dr. Oates then pointed out that the birth process is a symbol of the paradox of results. The natural abortion is an example of this. The mother was no failure as a mother, but the natural processes of life were succeeding in getting a negative result. Dr. Hayes illustrated the idea with the high value of a negative result in a physical examination. These mean more than if the doctor had found something actually wrong. The patient would be in terrible jeopardy if a doctor judged himself in terms of finding a disease; if a doctor judged himself as a success in terms of always finding a disease, he would be a dangerous doctor. The Taoist proverb, "By not doing, all things are accomplished," sums up the minus factor in initiative.

Dr. Oates pointed out that if Mr. Boyer had forced the issue, he would have failed and that it took considerable paradoxical intention to reverse the initiative. He told the parable of trying to "help" an egg to hatch. It takes a reverse of effort to let the egg hatch. This is a paradox of initiative epitomized in the Oriental proverb: "By not doing, all things are accomplished." Thus, any fully orbed view of initiative must take into consideration this degree of ambiguity in the whole problem.

Mr. Boyer in his own evaluation of this situation at the end of the seminar said that the situation "called for restraint on my part in moving toward Mr. M. This restraint did elicit a response from him. Dr. Hayes said that my entrance into Mr. M.'s world caused him to work harder in his psychotherapy with Dr. Hayes. My simply standing firm with a minus value of initiative rather than moving toward him may have given him something to push against, thus propelling him closer to Dr. Hayes. If I had moved toward him too much, I might have pushed him out of Dr. Hayes's care. My first conclusion, as experienced in the course, is that I must always be as sensitive to this dual function as I relate to people in my ministry."

The above account illustrates the minus, or passive, dimension of initiative. In my opinion the major contribution of psychiatry and psychology to pastoral counseling in the first three quarters of the twentieth century has been to teach us the disciplines of letting nature and God cure while we assist and comfort by providing *presence* and reducing loneliness and hopelessness by that presence.

"Plus" Factors in the Tools of Initiative

The second observation about initiative goes beyond the amount of effort it takes to serve the Lord by "standing and waiting." Decisions are made to move *toward* a person, to stimulate his sense of need, to remove a hidden agenda of nonverbal awareness that something is wrong. Action is taken. Initiative has its plus factor as well.

The assumptions of the medical-psychiatric model of a minus factor in initiative, however, do not embrace the needs of persons who are not sick in any clinically definable sense of the word "sick." Nor does the passive model of care and counseling consider the nature of *some* illnesses. The depressed person *by the nature of depression itself,* for example, cannot take initiative. He does not feel worthy of the time and attention of others. He assumes often that no one could care for a person like him. The publican who saw himself as a sinner did not even dare look up and speak to God in prayer. Therefore crisis intervention has become a form of initiative even within the fields of psychiatry and medicine in general. The exertion of initiative has become more a part of the "medical model" itself.

For example, Gerald Caplan has provided a model of preventive psychiatry based on the community intervention at specific times of crisis in people's lives. The provision of a life-support system of neither too much nor too little emotional "supplies" effectively deters the possibility of mental disorder. This concept of intervention has been implicit in the great rituals of Judaism, in the confessional in Catholicism, and in pastoral visitation in the Protestant tradition. However, the psychological depths of these ministries is only now beginning to be appreciated in pastoral counseling. They are built-in opportunities for inquiry and initiative on the part of rabbi, priest, or minister. I have espoused this use of traditional expectations of clergymen since the beginning of my work in the field of pastoral counseling in 1943. The initiative a clergyman takes through his *expected* ministries is more often interpreted by parishioners as considerateness and awareness of them as persons. The lack of such initiative is often interpreted as either inexperience, insensitivity, or laziness. Laziness is the pejorative term for undue passivity! (See Gerald Caplan, *Principles of Preventive Psychiatry*, pp. 31 ff., Basic Books, Inc., 1964; and Wayne Oates, *The Christian Pastor*, rev. ed., pp. 1–42; The Westminster Press, 1964.)

The clergyman of today has more tools at his disposal than the traditional ones of the rituals, the confessional, and pastoral visitation. These are obvious tools, neglected and misused, but other tools are available to the clergyman.

When one does or does not take initiative, he *does* something. He acts. Through the centuries of man's interaction with his fellows, certain acts have become ritualized into rather concrete "tools" of initiative that a pastor may use when he does exercise aggressive initiative and move toward a person. The particular tool of initiative is calibrated to an *amount* of aggression. My point is that a given pastoral situation can be assessed. A relatively precise decision can be made as to how much aggression the pastor can employ if he knows which tools are available. Each instrument represents a different degree of initiative. These tools can be identified as follows:

1. *The Act of Noticing.* The minister exerts initiative with his capacity to observe people. He watches their behavior as assiduously as he listens to what they say. He may exert a "minus factor of initiative" when he does *not* make verbal response to noticing that a young teen-age boy has cut his long hair when, to this moment, it has been a subject of conflict between him and his parents. The minister exerts a minus initiative when he does *not* make reference to the fact that a certain student is the son or daughter of a prominent churchman, politician, or entertainer. He expresses "plus factors of initiative" when he does make notice verbally of a shy and withdrawn church member who comes in to church late, leaves early, and makes few friends. He does so again when he notices an individual's handmade art object, a piece of apparel, or a bit of his writing. He notices an unusual effort to follow what he is saying in a sermon by remarking: "I appreciated the way you listened. It helped me to do a better job of preaching." He notices changes in behavior, appearance, and companions. He notices things other people fail to see, appreciate, marvel at, or understand.

Jesus *noticed* Zacchaeus, a short man who had gone to the trouble to climb a tree to see Jesus for himself. He noticed the woman with an issue of blood as she touched his garment. He noticed fishermen at their nets, a woman drawing water at a well, and a helpless man struggling to wash himself in reputedly healing waters. The pastoral counselor can exercise this initiative as a continuing principle of pastoral counseling. As Henry T. Close says of his counselee: "To build myself into another person's life, we need to become important to each other. I look for things in him that will make him interesting to me, that will help me to value him. And I look for opportunities to invest something of myself in him—feelings, associations, fantasies, etc." ("Three Basic Principles in Pastoral Counseling," *Pastoral Psychology,* Vol. XXIII, No. 227, October

1972, p. 13.) Such "looking" calls for the initiative of noticing; *paying* attention costs something. It is a form of initiative.

2. *The Act of Greeting*. Another degree of initiative is represented in the act of greeting persons, speaking to them before being spoken to by them. Carrying on a conversation after speaking to them takes more initiative than simply passively responding when spoken to. To take more initiative and greet the person in the elevator, the one who shares a taxi to the airport, the one who rarely comes out the door where the "official greeters" are, the one walking dejectedly down a school corridor, calls for energy of being on the part of anyone. The act of greeting, together with its meanings, varies from one area of a country to another and from one country to another.

In Eric Berne's transactional analysis the act of greeting is called "stroking." Rather than depend upon withdrawal as a way of handling short-term structures of time in social interaction, people have developed safe forms of interaction stylized into rituals that convey little information but carry the power of mutual recognition. These units of recognition are predictably packaged. Berne calls these units "strokes," and they are programmed by tradition and social custom. For example, one stroke is to greet another person by saying: "Good morning." A second stroke is: "How are you today?" A third one would be: "I've missed seeing you. Have you been away and are you O.K.?" Berne suggests that saying "Hello" is not easy. It takes getting rid of all the trash that has been programmed into your head since birth and knowing instead that "this particular Hello will never happen again." Getting rid of the trash in your head enables you "to see that there is somebody standing there or walking by, waiting for you to say hello back." To greet another calls for continuing to push out all the trash that keeps coming back into your head: "all the after-burns of all the grievances you have experienced and all the reach-backs of all the troubles you are planning to get into." Being able to say "Hello" is a way of learning to greet another person genuinely and with no ulterior motive, not with a superficial hello, not with a tense and sympathetic hello, but with a relaxed and real hello. (Eric Berne, *What Do You Say After You've Said Hello?* pp. 2, 4, 6; Grove Press, Inc., 1972.) A genuine greeting calls for personal discipline and an extension of oneself. If it is real, it becomes a treasure.

3. *The Act of Remembering.* To remember someone's name and call him by it when you meet him again is a massive act of initiative. For many years in my school we had an eloquent personality who served as registrar, dean of students, director of admissions, and personal counselor. It took at least four persons to replace him when he retired. Yet in his uniqueness a certain charisma was and is irreplaceable. He could remember every student's name because he studied all the students' names and pictures before they arrived. He is unforgettable because of the massive amount of energy he expended in remembering people.

The pastoral counselor can keep careful records that refresh his memory before he sees a counselee again. Yet his remembering the unique things that particular counselee has told him, the unusually profound things he has learned from that counselee, and the not-so-obvious strengths of that counselee is a way of demonstrating initiative, being active, getting involved creatively in the flowing direction of the counselee's life.

Sometimes the act of remembering can take on the form of a lasting ritual. In the room in my home where I work is an array of tiny symbols of counselees of years gone by. Among them is a decoupaged handful of jonquils. They are reminiscent of a young man who was treacherously depressed. It was in late December and mid-winter. I dared to say to him and his wife: "I predict and I pray that you will be well by the time the jonquils bloom in Kentucky." He was. Sometime later the picture with nothing but their names on the package came to me in the mail. Reminiscence works both ways as a form of initiative in the movement of persons toward each other.

Coupled with the here-and-now initiative of remembrance of the pastoral counselor is his necessary awareness of the importance of anniversaries for both celebration (such as the coming of the jonquils) and consolation (such as the anniversary of a death, a divorce, an imprisonment of a person, etc.). The pastoral counselor who would "tend to his flock" is advised to "show up" by letter, telephone, visit, or scheduled interview on or near the anniversary of either a tragedy or a time for celebration, such as the anniversary of a divorce or the anniversary of a wedding that he performed. A recent study of the dynamics of the alienation of persons from the church through hostile rejection of its pastor and program showed that such rejection was most often triggered by his failure to remember with the passage of time to provide specific ministries of remembrance and follow-up to people who had lost someone by death or by divorce or who had been retired from their jobs. (Daniel Bagby, "A Phenomenological Approach to the Pastoral Care of Selected Alienated Church Members in a Local Baptist Church." Unpublished doctoral dissertation, Southern Baptist Theological Seminary, 1973.) Just one or two expressions of initiative were ineffective. Such persons, however, were uniformly open to and somewhat surprised by the initiative taken by the person doing the research. They felt remembered, not forgotten.

4. *The Act of Writing.* One of the oldest and most venerable tools of initiative is the letter. Paul wrote to Philemon in Onesimus' behalf. Much of the New Testament is composed of letters, some called *pastoral* epistles. The pastor today, for example, is repetitively faced with marriage-counseling situations in which one partner comes to him but the other does not. One way of taking initiative without invading the privacy of the other spouse and without *demanding* a response is to write a letter to the person inviting him or her to participate in the process of understanding and ministering to the needs of the spouse who did come for help. This also does away with a secret agenda between the pastor and the spouse who came for counseling. Whether the person comes for counseling

or not, the pastor has acted responsibly and refused to deal with the mate clandestinely.

The act of writing a letter opens up the possibility of a correspondence ministry. Additional help, coupled with "free writing" as a supplement to counseling, may be to get the counselee to keep a diary, to write poetry, or to write essays. Charles Kemp points to the advantages and uses of these tools as being helpful (a) when counseling is interrupted, (b) when more sessions are needed than time permits, (c) when the waiting period for the first interview or for later interviews is too long. I would add to these the use of writing when the person comes a long distance for help, or when the person is more articulate in writing than in speaking.

Of course, as Kemp indicates, writing is not an option with persons who do not like to write. With those too young to write, art and drawing sometimes work. For example, I corresponded with a six-year-old child through her mother. As the child grew, she would draw a picture of her hand to show me how much she had grown. Conversely, some pastoral counselors abhor writing letters and prefer to use the telephone. Writing is a tool of chance, but the idiosyncrasies of both the counselee and the counselor condition its value. When it is used, however, it represents a low degree of initiative that is often highly adaptable to many situations. As Kemp says, writing continues the demonstration of care and concern when time is almost nonexistent. Writing provides self-understanding and reduces tension. Writing provides both the counselee and the counselor with a record of what was said. (Charles Kemp, "The Use of Free Writing as a Supplement to Pastoral Counseling," *The Journal of Pastoral Care,* Vol. XXVII, No. 1, March 1973, pp. 26–29.)

One of the most helpful uses of the letter, I have found, is that a counselee can keep the letter and read it many times. It refreshes the memory of the person as to *what* the counselor *did* say. For example, the memory of elderly people, of patients under heavy sedation, and of patients undergoing shock treatment is clouded and impaired (though not permanently in the last two instances). A letter constitutes a fresh conversation or visit with them. I have been awed at the length of time some persons have kept the letters that I have written to them.

5. *The Act of Telephoning.* The telephone is an instrument of initiative that is looked upon either as an idol or as a slave-master or as both by many persons. Yet it is here to stay. The effective use of the telephone in pastoral care and counseling can be to the pastor as a brush is to the artist. The technology of the telephone for the pastoral counselor is worthy of extensive research. Several hypotheses for research can be set forth here.

First, the telephone provides a means of conversing with people without observing their body language. They can be reached in the privacy of their homes and spared the struggle that getting dressed and making an office visit requires. The pastor can provide them and himself with all the advantages Freud spoke of in psychoanalysis when he sat out of sight of the patient. It has the advantage of the confessional booth. This relative degree of anonymity may heighten, and it certainly conditions, the kind and quality of communication.

Second, for the person who is prone to forget or to break appointments or for the one who is simply unaccustomed to making appointments, a telephone call prior to the time of appointment, as a reminder, helps offset this. Dentists, for example, have a ritual of the "reminder telephone call." One study showed that chronic alcoholics had a higher rate of recovery when their appointments were both preceded and followed by a telephone call, the first one as a reminder and the one later as an expression of concern. (Morris E. Chafetz *et al.,* eds., *Frontiers of Alcoholism,* pp. 67–70; Science House, Inc., 1970.)

Third, the telephone call can reduce the possibility of confusing a relationship. A pastor who visits the home of a divorcée or a widow can hardly do so appropriately very many times in succession. However, a brief telephone call can reduce the possibility of misunderstanding and can deal specifically with recurrent problems.

Fourth, the telephone conversation can be a way of providing security for the person who is easily overwhelmed by the bodily presence of a pastor. A very shy young boy or girl, usually in the years from ten to fifteen, will quite often find it easier to talk on the telephone than in an office visit or a home visit. I recall being of continuing assistance to an eleven-year-old girl whose father had committed suicide. She could communicate with comfort over the phone, whereas a home visit was a "state occasion" to the whole family. She has never been in my office, but she has visited me at my home.

Fifth, the telephone can be a "slender thread" between a pastoral counselor and a severely depressed and potentially suicidal person. Of course, one should seek to align these persons with both their family physician and a psychiatrist, but many such persons have to wait for appointments. Even when they are under the care of a physician, the pastoral counselor dare not "ditch" or "desert" them. Therefore, he can take the initiative and call them periodically. He can even make appointments as to *when* he will call. He can ask them to call him when they feel the temptation to commit suicide coming strongly upon them. He can ask them to promise him that they will call him at any time.

Finally, the pastor can unwittingly become the person whom the chronic and repetitive telephone caller compulsively calls. This person's use of the telephone is an unstudied mystery in its own right. My experiences with nine such counselees have been somewhat dismal; my observations showed that they were people who were alone in the world; they survived fairly well when working but tended to fall apart emotionally when they went back to an empty house. They, with one exception, were men or women who had no close ties of mutuality with anyone. Their relationships were "one-way" relationships: alternately they were either supervising or helping other people or they were parasitically dependent on another. They could not both minister to and be ministered to by the same person. As a pastoral counselor, I wound up in the position of being 100 percent "helper" to a 100 percent helper.

More recently, I have discovered that a frank covenant of a two-way reciprocity was needed. This could come in the form of setting a specific, limited time when such people called me. This met their needs and did not dominate my office time or my evenings at home. The two-way contract could come in the form of money for the support and care of students of mine. Thus I became a "broker" between their need to be helped and their propensity to help others but not me. My most recent experiences seem to point in the direction of the latter formula for enabling the person to maintain his dignity, to get the support and counsel he needs, and to respect my limits of time and energy as a human being.

6. *The Visit*. The higher degrees of pastoral initiative appear in home visits or hospital visits. Such visits can be of two varieties: the prearranged visit and the unannounced visit. The latter represents more initiative than the former and has the advantage, or disadvantage, of the element of surprise. The visit can best be understood in the light of the motives or purposes of the pastor in making the call. As such, the varieties of visits can be identified as follows:

a. *The "putting in an appearance" visit*. The pastor visits because it is expected or requested of him. He has no internal motivation for making the call. This is the least motivation he can have. Because this type outnumbers most other visits, many ministers think of visiting as a thing "not for them."

b. *The social visit*. The pastor makes this call simply to get acquainted, to be a part of a social occasion such as a reception, a tea, or a party, or to see these people just because they are friends.

c. *The crisis visit*. The pastor may visit at this time in relation to his counseling task. A crisis such as an illness, a death, an accident, a divorce in the family, a son going to war, etc., provides a time of deepening and opening of relationships. As such the visit may be a form of precounseling initiative when openings are made and plans are laid for a continuous counseling relationship in the pastor's office.

d. *The celebration visit*. Here the pastor helps a young

couple celebrate moving into their first apartment or buying a new house or the birth of a baby. He helps an older couple with the send-off of a son or a daughter to college, a sixteenth birthday, or whenever their teen-ager becomes the possessor of a driver's license. Except for the birth of a baby, these occasions are times when the organized church or the synagogue has few significant rituals. The clergyman can provide informal rituals by taking initiative at such times. These occasions give opportunity for the building of a trusted relationship to the clergyman that will be available in the event of a severe, negative, or emergency crisis. As Edward Thornton says, pastoral counseling can even take conflictual events as opportunities for creative growth. (*Theology and Pastoral Counseling*, pp. 112–113; Prentice-Hall, Inc., 1964.)

e. *The confrontation visit.* The pastor works in the open community without the controls that a hospital, a prison, a school, or even a community mental health system has. Yet persons for whom he is responsible do things that "make tidal waves" of reaction in the open community. These acts are reported to the pastor by people who in various ways say, "Do something." The person in question, however, will not come for help. He resists all overtures and appropriate initiative. The data the pastor has may range from idle gossip, to persistent rumor, to "soft data" the pastor knows to be true but cannot move on because it is not demonstrable evidence, to hard fact, such as when one of his church members is actually convicted in a court of law for embezzlement. In all such instances, the person does not ask for pastoral assistance.

The pastor's position, therefore, is one in which he takes the greatest degree of initiative possible, risks total rejection, and meets the person. He may tell the person, briefly and to the point, that the truth or the error of what is being said in the open community is not his concern. Rather, his concern is the well-being and the happiness of the person himself. If the things being said are *not* true, they nevertheless hurt and hinder the well-being and happiness of the person himself. The pastor can define his role as neither detective, nor jury, nor judge, but as pastor, confidant, and friend. If the person chooses to let the pastor be a confidant and friend, he can be sure that the pastor will be highly responsible and will not discuss the data given without first conferring with the person himself. However, the pastor can say that he simply is standing at the person's door and knocking. He will not invade the privacy of the person. The person must open the door and let the pastor in.

INITIATIVE AND SOCIAL ACTION

Such instances represent the most common problems of confrontation that a pastor meets. Less common but maybe more significant are those times when the pastor faces huge social injustices, finds the persons in power responsible, and goes to them as a man of God to see if relief and justice cannot be effected. He may find that one of his fellow ministers has been arrested in a protest meeting and jailed for a felony when actually—from a legal point of view—what he did was a misdemeanor. He may discover that the person who issued the warrants of arrest is a member of his own congregation. He then may go to this person and appeal to his own better judgment that these charges should be dropped. Such use of initiative moves our discussion into the area of the private and public ministry of a pastor, the role of the pastoral counselor as an agent of social change and confrontation. Suffice it to say here that taking such initiative is both a part of and compatible with the role of the pastor as a counselor. Confrontation is a necessary part of even a reconciliation model of the pastor as a change agent. The deeper question is whether reconciliation is a necessary part of the punitive model of the pastor as a change agent. The punitive model, as used here, implies that the pastor uses political power to make a person or an organizational structure "wish they had" done as he suggested. Boycotts, political campaigning, the use of mass media publicity, protest marching, and the commandeering of property and even hostages are a few punitive tools of social change.

Ordinarily, the pastor as a counselor is a man of understanding who invites people to come to him and reason together with the hope that contending parties will find a common ground of information and that communication will be catalyzed. Thus, problems are often resolved through reconciliation. When this is not possible, then the pastor as a "reconciler" makes his appeal for an effective compromise in which contending parties "give in" *some* and gain *some* of the things they wanted. Yet even this fails in many polarized situations. Then the pastor as a counselor has two alternatives.

First, he can withdraw and turn the whole process over to the natural outcome of warring factions in the outworking of what may be called theologically the wrath of God and/or the direct intervention of the Holy Spirit. This is where most persons trained in pastoral counseling would tend to leave things. I am aware that my own book *Pastoral Counseling in Social Problems* leaves this clear impression even though in actual practice I went farther in social change. I did not consider what I did beyond this to be pastoral counseling in the technical sense of the word. What I did beyond the reconciliation model of pastoral counseling I classified in my own mind as "the use of political power by the pastor." It was not the pastor as counselor but the pastor as politician.

Since 1966, however, persons such as Robert Bonthius and Harvey Cox have said to me that their objection to pastoral counseling is that it is aimed at "adjusting people to unhealthy systems and structures." They ask for what they call activistic initiative to change the whole structural system in which the person lives. Such challenges must be taken seriously and challenged in return.

The pastoral counseling movement has been heavily engaged in changing the structures of society that care for the mentally disturbed, the delinquent, the alcoholic, the divorcée, and the sexual offender. Although our track record is good here, it is not good on the ministry to the poor and on the challenge of economic structures of property ownership. It is poor on our public participation in the race issue. It is better, thanks to the counter culture, on ecology. We have yet to be tested on women's rights, and there has been a strange silence among us on premarital counseling since the sexual revolution of the mid-sixties. The ministry of trained pastoral counselors in any concerted way on such problems as those of equal opportunity employment and payment for women— even in our own institutions—is dismally poor. We have even contributed to the segregation of the aged by our implicit assumption that "counseling is not indicated" for arteriosclerotic patients, for example.

Yet Bonthius and Cox both reveal the untoward effects of some—but not all—training in pastoral counseling. Some education in counseling overidentifies it as (a) the main and only thing a pastor does and (b) identical with client-centered psychotherapy, where the counselor is passive and not confrontational. I would challenge this and say that I have always seen counseling as one of the things a pastor does. The pastor is also a citizen and a prophetic challenger of the defective structures around him. He is under obligation to assess the political processes going on around him, to identify the social and ethical issues at stake, to marshal political "clout," and to use it when it is necessary. I have always seen this as my responsibility, have used political power wherever it was ethically available, and have done so both publicly and privately.

The real issue involved here is not the opinions of pastoral counselors vis-à-vis social activists. The real issues are as to when a pastor should work privately and when he should resort to preaching, writing for the newspapers, speaking on radio and television, and becoming a part of public protest movements. In both instances, private and public, he uses political power or clout. As a rule, I have not been averse to using it (a) when I had such power, (b) when I could mobilize it, and (c) when it was calculated actually to get pragmatic results quite apart from publicity for my own "image." To demonstrate what I mean the next chapter is devoted to the ambiguity between the private and the public ministry of the pastor. Suffice it to say here that there is a time when a pastor consciously and intentionally uses political power in a model that could be called "punitive." Such action fits admirably the behavior modification concept of negative reinforcement.

A THEOLOGICAL PERSPECTIVE OF INITIATIVE

The passive model of ministry is essentially an Olympian view of the nature of God and what God expects of us as the extended Shadow of the Divine. The Olympian view perceives man as having to storm the ramparts of heaven and steal the fire with which to survive, whether in anger or in love or both. The servant of God accordingly enjoys his own Olympus until someone almost reaches his level and dares to ask for help. Then the relationship tends to be an "over-under" or "helper-helped" relationship. In its most extreme form this Olympian outlook denies the humanity of the counselor and overemphasizes that of the counselee. It could well lead to a private game that the powerful and the powerless play with each other.

The aggressive model has some of the same pitfalls. It is a sort of Hound of Heaven view of the nature of God and what God expects of man. Here man sits and waits for God to act, to take initiative toward him. Extreme distortions of Calvinism have interpreted God as the one and the only one who could do anything to intervene in behalf of a person. As a result the person in need never becomes a counselee. He sits and waits for the visitation of God. The idea of his being a "seeker" after God is foreign to him. God seeks him. No act of exerted faith is required of him.

When, however, one discovers the common element of initiative in both aggressiveness (the plus factor of initiative) and passivity (the minus factor of initiative) an incarnational view of God's intentions emerges. God does take initiative in prophets and wise persons. He does so fully in the Messiah. The Messiah comes as the one who takes the form of those whom he serves. He nevertheless does not override the integrity, individuality, and power of decision of a person. He requires initiative in exerted acts of faith. He stands at the door and knocks. We open, and he comes in and dines with us. He presents reality to us, but he permits us to go away sorrowing if we are bound up with inferior but prior loyalties. He asks us to stretch forth our hand, to take up our bed and walk, or to go show ourselves to the priest. It is reciprocity and two-way covenant all the way.

Chapter 8

THE PRIVATE AND
THE PUBLIC MINISTRY

The pastor as a counselor is not *just* a private counselor. What he does in private as a counselor is always in tension with his responsibility as a public figure, a public speaker, a person with corporate and community responsibilities. He is ordinarily employed by a congregation, serves a parachurch institution, or is legally required to be answerable to an ecclesiastical body through ordination. This latter legal requirement is made by state governments and the Federal Government in their employment of ministers as chaplains, for example.

A case in point is the struggle for social change that we had in the 1940's and 1950's to wrest the appointment of chaplains from the political patronage system. A merit system appointment on the basis of professional training for the chaplaincy has, as a result of this struggle, become the prevailing mode of action in many state and federal institutions. Yet, in the late 1960's, when public protest and the use of political exposure in print and on television became the techniques of choice for social change, some chaplains felt that they should use these procedures to change things in the Establishment that they considered evil. Then they were confronted by administrators telling them that theirs were nonpolitical appointments and that this also implied that they themselves were not to engage in politics beyond casting their own secret ballot! They could not have it both ways. In such a dilemma the chaplain would have to rely on the political process apart from his own neutrality or he would have to earn his living apart from state funds and conduct his public campaigns as an outsider. This subtle ambiguity was doubly difficult for some clinical pastoral education students to see because ordinarily they were not being paid. Yet they *were*, in effect, guests of the Establishment and could be told to leave at any time.

Nevertheless, individuals and small groups call upon their pastors, some of whom are chaplains in institutions, for counsel. Here the pastor's influence can be felt privately but not seen publicly. When people turn to him for any reason, they expect a measure of privacy. Therefore, the pastor's private ministry to individuals and groups is set within the context of his public ministry, which in turn is nourished and/or blighted by his private ministry. He is both consciously and unconsciously directed by the heavy tension that is produced by the ambiguity between the private and the public aspects of ministry.

"I Want a Private Pastor!"

The tension I am describing I first felt consciously in 1951. An active and loyal member of a church of another denomination came to me for counseling. She said that her pastor was a competent counselor and a helpful preacher. Both she and her husband held offices in the congregational governance. I asked why it was she came to me—a total stranger—when she seemed to trust her pastor greatly. She replied that it was not a matter of trust, but that he simply could not provide the amount of privacy she needed. To involve him in her troubles would only be to complicate them as much as to talk with a member of her family. Then she said, "I want a *private* pastor." In this story rests some of the dynamics of the emergence of pastoral counseling as a subgrouping of the ministry. Some of these dynamics can be extrapolated here.

The Fear of Exposure

The woman valued her pastor's approval as a working member of his church. The fear of his disapproval and the possible disqualification of herself in the work of the church caused her to take her private burdens elsewhere. Ambiguously enough, her private problems and her public responsibilities worked at cross-purposes with each other. Consequently, she settled the tension by getting one minister to meet her private needs while continuing to rely upon another minister in her durable, public needs. Yet, as a minister who keeps protesting that the private and the public ministries of a pastor cannot be separated, I myself was observing before my own eyes the two being neatly separated in the conscious thinking of a counselee who has continued to be a responsible member of her church for the twenty-two years since!

Already veteran pastors will ask: "Did you not have the ethical responsibility to advise her pastor that a member of his congregation was consulting with you?" Such a question makes me squirm. I feel that I had an ethical obligation to strengthen and not to undermine her relationship to her church. This I have done, and it *was* strengthened. In this sense I felt obligated to him. With the resolution of some of her stress, she told him herself after conferring with me about it. I encouraged her to tell him, and the telling strengthened our relationship to each other as fellow ministers. If she had not chosen to tell him herself, my own response to her need for a private pastor would have kept me from mentioning it to him. The fact is that he knows nothing as yet about what I heard her discuss. Neither does anyone else. Hence, the threat of exposure was removed both from her dialogue and from mine.

The Need for Confession. This woman had a burden of private loss, fear, inhibition, and anger that she needed to disburden. None of it involved anyone in her family or the extended

family of her church. She was fiercely loyal to them. In Kierkegaard's fine words, her burden involved memories and decisions of "the self in relation to itself" and to God. But she
needed a private pastor to be an alter ego in her soul's soliloquy
and in her prayers before God. Ideally, her pastor *could* have
provided this. Pragmatically, she felt otherwise. This realm
of privacy in her own being was something no one, and no
church, could program. She chose a private pastor to meet her
need for disburdening and for spiritual direction. The private,
confessional dimension of life is both traditionally and neo-
traditionally an unquenchable demand of persons and also apt
to be exploited and commercialized. The reactivation of an
informal but deeply personal ministry of confession is perennially needed in and out of the church.

Consequently, pastoral counseling itself has absorbed much
of what in highly liturgical churches is called "the confessional." Churches without a ritual of confession have been most
active in the development of pastoral counseling. (See Max
Thurian, *Confession,* London: SCM Press, Ltd., 1958; and also
Edward Thurneysen, *A Theology of Pastoral Care,* John Knox
Press, 1962.) Data confided in the confessional relationship
are not given to the minister himself. He is permitted to "over-
hear" them as the person gives them to God. He is an enabler
of the person's prayers, not the primary recipient of information. Such data therefore are now, as always, sacrosanct and
told to no one by the minister. The high tradition of ministry
at the distinctly confessional level is not to be shared with
anyone but God. No one who has not developed a confessional-
level relationship with the person has any right to know what
was said. Therefore, if anyone is to tell what was said, the
person who made the confession is the one to do it. Herein is
where the line between the confessional and pastoral counseling—even though it is a moving line—must be drawn and
redrawn. It involves the consequences of the persons themselves talking with others, not merely the pastor "breaking
confidences."

The whole issue of the legal aspects of the protection of the

pastor as a counselor from being used as a witness in court
has been thoroughly discussed in William Harold Tremann's
book *The Right to Silence* (John Knox Press, 1964). Until
now this has been more of a moot issue than a repetitive problem. In nearly thirty years of pastoral work, I have been faced
with the possibility of subpoena only once. With pastoral counseling vying for place as a health delivery specialty, however,
this will become increasingly more real as the pastoral counselor becomes more dependent upon fees for services rendered
in a contractual way, as is characteristic of other health delivery professions.

The more prevalent issues, however, in private communications with counselees are interpersonal rather than legal,
covenantal rather than contractual. The person who comes for
counseling to his pastor or to some other minister, as in the
case above, usually is suffering from isolation and fear of
rejection by others. He may or may not have done things about
which he does not wish others to know. He may or may not
want the fact that he has sought assistance from the pastor
to be known to others. On the other hand, the pastor accepts a
measure of responsibility for the counselee's "story." Just knowing some things is a heavy load to carry, especially when a
pastor is responsible to the church as well as to the individual.
On both sides, the pastor and the counselee live under the
threat of exposure. How can this threat be removed? It can
best be removed by the establishment of a *covenant of communication.*

A covenant of communication is much more than a promise
not to tell anything the person has said, which may or may
not be a wise thing to promise. A covenant of communication
consists of a mutual understanding that both the counselor
and the counselee will consult with each other *before* either
of them discusses their conversation with anyone else. Thus,
no one is told what has been discussed without the permission
of the other to do so. Thus, information will fall into at least
three different categories depending upon the degree of the
threat of exposure inherent within the information. First, there

is *community knowledge*. The pastor receives information from the counselee that is commonly known in the community. Such information may be a matter of public record if it has appeared in the local newspapers. Or it may be known by a considerable number of other people and is therefore common information. Much that the unsuspecting pastor receives as confidential information is of just this order of knowledge. The person himself may have told this to many other people, each one having been told "in confidence." He probably has forgotten about these persons, and when one of them reminds him of it he is likely to think that the pastor has betrayed him. Consequently, it is standard clinical procedure for the pastor to find out to whom else the counselee has talked about his problem.

Second, there is *privileged communication*. This is information which the pastor or the counselee may pass on if the other gives him the privilege of doing so. Usually this is the kind of privilege which is granted for the communication of necessary information to other professional people who may be called upon as referral sources. Sharing data with another professional person also distributes the burden of responsibility to more persons than just the pastor. It lowers his own sense of isolation and anxiety. Case conferences among professional people fall into this category of relationships in the use of information. The main feature of this is that privilege is granted only when necessity prevails. The question arises as to whether a pastor's wife should know about his counseling relationships. Quite often it is necessary for her to know in order that she may accept her share of responsibility or in order that she may react appropriately in behalf of the counselee at times. But it is not always necessary, and when necessity does arise, the counselee should be consulted beforehand.

However, the pastor needs to be extremely careful how much and how quickly he accepts such confidences. The person who too quickly disburdens too much may be shocked at himself for doing so and may be reluctant to sustain the counseling relationship as a result. Also, if the counselee confides in another person, the pastor has the right to know who that person is if the necessity arises. He should at some time or other in the relationship make this clear to the counselee. This is a part of the reciprocal nature of the covenant of communication. If effectively established and clearly accepted, such a covenant tends to remove the threat of exposure.

Such a covenant as has just been described mutually allocates responsibility to the counselor and to the counselee. But this uncovers another threat: *the threat of irresponsibility.* Talking with other people outside the counseling relationship can be done either in a responsible or in an irresponsible way. This is also true of other aspects of the relationship. For example, the pastor may have made it very clear that an effective counseling situation must be carried on in his office under discreetly private conditions. A given counselee, however, may insist upon turning every social occasion into a rehearsal of personal problems. All the while he avoids making an appointment to deal more formally with them. Furthermore, the person who comes for the interview may distort what was actually said in the interview and leave on the community impressions severely threatening to the pastor. The pastor, in turn, may be panicky at hearing the nature of the problems the person has to tell and so may make a referral before his own relationship has deepened enough for his word about the referral to be understood. He may throw up his hands in helplessness and say, "There is nothing I can do to help you." On both sides of the encounter, irresponsibility can threaten the whole relationship.

The solid ground of mutually shared responsibility for dealing reciprocally with the problem must be established. The threat of irresponsibility must be faced and removed before any effective counseling actually takes place. In the event that this cannot be removed, the pastor should limit his relationship to that degree of responsibility which he can effectively discharge. For example, faced with the person who refuses to discuss his problem, except as an informal friend in social situations, the pastor can treat him as a supportive friend treats his friends but not as a person who is seriously attempting to deal responsibly with problems. Or the person, when he asks a blunt question, "What can I do about this?" can be told tactfully that there are persons in the community who can help him. He can be referred to other counselors. The pastor who is panicked by the story of a counselee can tell the person what he *can* do before he tells him what he cannot do. This gives support and removes threat.

THE PROCESS OF PASTORAL COUNSELING

Once precounseling initiatives have been taken and once the "roominess" of a private counseling relationship has been established, the process of pastoral counseling is on its way. A detailed description of this process is somewhat as follows.

The Phase of Participant Understanding

The establishment of a clear covenant of communication tends to develop an atmosphere of trust and security. As William Glasser says, the first step in any kind of counseling is for the counselor and the counselee to become responsible friends. Mutual responsibility provides a basis for both counselor and counselee treating each other as persons and not as means to some ulterior ends. Now they can participate with each other with understanding and purpose as they seek to resolve whatever difficulties the counselee is facing. They focus upon these difficulties. The counselor participates in the world view of the counselee to the limit of his vision. As Heidegger says, he allows the self of the counselee "to see from itself that which it shows itself, as it shows itself from itself." He empties himself of his own perspective and participates with understanding in the perspective of the counselee. He does not, for that matter, just sit and listen when what is being said is not really understood. He seeks to clarify what the person is saying in such a way that it means as nearly as is possible the same thing to the counselor that it means to the counselee.

Understanding Past and Present. The self-revelation of the counselee has a specific time reference. His conversations consist largely of an alternating penetration into present difficulties punctuated by intermittent flashbacks into the past. He discusses how things have always been in times past. All the while the present difficulties are being understood somewhat differently than before. The judgment of the present upon the past brings new interpretations to the times past, and vice versa. For example, the person is likely to say: "I used to think . . . , but now it looks different." During this phase of the dialogue, the pastor actively listens by letting the person talk, by providing undivided attention, and by insisting upon really understanding what the counselee means by what he says. A good measure of attention will be devoted in a later chapter to the nature and importance of the religious history. Suffice it to say here that the process of pastoral counseling consists in a measure of bringing the past and the present to focus realistically upon each other. This is not the abstract process of "getting facts" from the counselee; rather, it is the living process of participating in the interpretation and reinterpretation that present and past bring to each other.

Conflicts of Values. The pulling power of a participant kind of listening brings to the counselee's clear level of attention the excruciating conflicts in his value systems and in his feelings toward the people who represent these values in his life. He peers through an astringent, eye-smarting spiritual smog filled with the fumes of a technological culture. He tries to discern "between the things that differ," to sense what is vital, and to disentangle himself from the dead weight of what is not vital. He has to make decisions as to the validity of the way of life that led him to the plight in which he finds himself. He ponders the meaning of those acts which he committed that seemed at the time to be done by someone else and not by himself, a sort of "not me." Then he finds a kinship with his own acts that enables him to confess that in deed and in truth it was he who did them. For them *he* was responsible.

One little girl's mother scolded her, saying: "Mary! Only the devil could have made you push your little brother down the stairs and kick him in the face!" She replied: "The devil made me push him down the stairs, Mother. But kicking him in the face was my own idea!" If she had been a contemporary adult, she would probably have uttered some psychological truism such as: "An uncontrollable impulse got hold of me when my little brother came around, and Mother's rejection of me made it worse." She would have learned how to interpret her own experience in such a way as to avoid responsible decisions. In other words, she could say, "It was 'not me' but my parents who did this thing." But in the process of patient and participant listening, a decisive struggle is going on as to one's own responsibilities, the things he has done which are his own ideas. The conflict of values comes to the surface in the pastoral counseling relationship. The counselee runs a hard course between a darkened, compulsive, overscrupulous conscience on the one hand, and, on the other, the temptation to use the popular distortions of psychology and religion as a means of avoiding self-encounter, personal responsibility, and mature decisions.

Self-encounter. The acceptance of responsibility for oneself as one is involves making decisions as to the kind of person one really is. One meets oneself in the dialogue of pastoral counseling. This is true of both the counselee and the counselor. One learns of one's typical mode of life, one's characteristic ways of handling one's existence, one's own particular ways of reacting to life. We shall discuss this at length in the next chapter, also, and the detailed patterns of self-encounter provide avenues of understanding between counselor and counselee. The point that needs to be made here is that this self-encounter is *reciprocal* at every step of the way. The counselor and the counselee both bring a distinct pattern of life to the relationship. The counselor is a trained person, but his training has made him an unauthentic being if he simply "plays a role," "acts a part," or "poses" a certain way for effect. This is the fallacy of stereotyping one particular method of counseling as normative of all relationships. Counselors avoid real encounter with their counselees when in behalf of a given method they react in unnatural, unauthentic, or devised ways even in the counseling situation itself. This in itself is a form of masking or avoidance of encounter.

Another aspect of this needs to be emphasized. To be one's genuine self without retreat behind an assumed "pose" makes one vulnerable indeed. The vulnerability of the self involves risk in the encounter. Yet without this vulnerability, the counselee does not learn to meet himself as in deed and in fact he really is. Consequently, the process of self-encounter is more often short-circuited by focusing upon "problems," by shadowboxing with ideological positions, and by retreating behind one stereotype after another. This kind of self-avoidance can also be reciprocal in such a way that no genuine conversation ever really takes place. This kind of studied avoidance of self-encounter particularly abounds in premarital pastoral counseling. The minister may see himself as a "friend of the family," as a "functionary of the church or state," as a counselor whose task it is to participate in the processes of understanding of the meaning of marriage. The couple may see him only as incidental to the whole procedure, as spiritual guide and interpreter of the meaning of their marriage, or as a person who asks too many embarrassing questions. Probably no particular kind of counseling which a pastor does is as fraught with as much avoidance of real self-encounter as premarital counseling.

But the decision to "face up to oneself" is in itself a turning point in the counseling relationship. This marks a "wheeling about" of direction in the processes of understanding. One has really taken hold of the resolving, deciding, and determining powers with which he is endowed. A definite converting of direction in his life has set in. At the very core of our need to *solve* problems is the prior necessity that the counselee *resolve* to meet himself. The counselor can provide the atmosphere in which this can take place. He can wait patiently while it takes place. But he cannot make this resolution *for* the counselee. Only the counselee himself can do this. A large part of the inner wisdom of counseling rests in the patience of the counselor to wait this out and the skill with which he maintains the confidence of the counselee while waiting. Once the counselee has resolved to encounter himself as he really is, however, the relationship moves into a new phase called the covenant-making phase of counseling.

The Covenant-making Phase

Binswanger and others emphasize that by nature man, as a "person-who-is-responsible-for-his-existence," chooses. (Rollo May and others, eds., *Existence*, p. 41; Basic Books, Inc., 1958.) In other words, man is capable of awareness of his own existence, feels responsible for his existence, and makes choices as to what he is going to do with his life. On the other hand, Martin Buber and Richard Niebuhr speak of man as a "promise-making, promise-keeping, promise-breaking being, as a man of faith" (H. Richard Niebuhr, *Radical Monotheism and Western Culture*, p. 41; Harper & Brothers, 1960). One can go farther and say in these two respects that the image of God in man becomes vividly clear: God himself is a responsible God and in history has made the decision to be in Christ. He makes promises and keeps them. He makes covenants, in other words. He relates himself to man within these covenants. The supreme covenant is the New Covenant in Jesus Christ.

The distinct characteristic of pastoral counseling is that the covenant-making responsibility of man and the covenant of faith in God provide the focal center of the meaning of the counseling. The Spirit of God works within man both to will and to do God's good pleasure. A covenant within an individual or a group begins forming deep in the recesses of the unconscious. This covenant is consciously focused upon the frustration that persons are suffering. It focuses and refocuses several times before the consummatory covenant is formed. These events of concentration may be called covenants in themselves in a progression of spiritual maturity. They are the covenant of confrontation, the covenant of confession, the covenant of forgiveness and restitution, and the covenant of concern. All of them require responsible and adult decision on the part of the individual or the group.

The Covenant of Confrontation. The choice between fantasy and reality is made at the inmost recesses of a person's being. This is a painfully difficult decision because there is always just enough of reality in any fantasy to make it seem "really" real. But the dreamlike quality of this reality is such that psychological mechanisms of isolation, projection, displacement, rationalization, and, most of all, repression, must be used to make up the difference between the world in which the person as a self exists and the world that exists around him in fact. Even apart from these more or less unconscious mechanisms, individuals and groups can deliberately and in cold blood be irresponsible and brutally unfeeling. The person (or the group) at some point takes a stand, makes a decision, and resolves to face life at it is and not as he would like to have it be. He chooses not to try to recast "the sorry scheme of things" after his own inner design. He faces up to life the way it is, with all its ambiguity, injustice, and frustration. This is really a covenant with oneself and with life itself. This covenant calls for courage, but the courage itself is an unmustered courage. This courage comes from the patience and understanding that the person has already received as he has been "understood" by God and by his pastor.

But simply understanding and being understood are not ends within themselves. They lay the groundwork and provide the courage whereby the individual is encouraged to make a covenant to confront life itself as it is. The forces of resolve are counteracted by other forces of resistance. A conflict rages. But the individual covenants—as Perls, Hefferline, and Goodman put it—"to stand out of the way, to give the threat all (his) powers, and . . . to relax useless deliberateness, to let the conflict rage and destroy what must be destroyed" (Frederick Perls, Ralph Hefferline, Paul Goodman, *Gestalt Therapy: Excitement and Growth in Human Personality,* p. 359; The Julian Press, Inc., 1951). This, put in Biblical terms, is like the prodigal son "coming to himself" and choosing, whatever the cost, to face life rather than to run from it, to encounter life as it is rather than to live in a dream world of imagination, however important and treasured the imagination may be.

The Covenant of Confession. In the phase of participant understanding, the counselee may have told the pastor many details about himself. But pastoral counseling is not just a matter of "getting the facts," of extracting a history, from the individual. These facts must be confronted on a deeper level of reality, and this takes time. The covenant of confrontation sets this process of "working through" into motion. Then the individual resolves to confess to God his own resolution to change. Until now his anxiety and guilt have been directed toward first one person and then another in his field of interpersonal relationships. The covenant of confrontation is followed by a resolve to relate these to God. The human idols whom the individual has both worshiped and desecrated are the sources and targets of anxiety and guilt. The covenant of confession transmutes anxiety and guilt into a clearly focused sense of sin in relation to God and God alone. This refocuses the whole perspective of the counselee. The things he considered as heinous wrongs before appear to be trivial now. The things he did not consider at all become great in his mind. Ethical seriousness, free of "gamesmanship," makes for ethical perspective.

The vast difference between anxiety and guilt, on the one hand, and a clear sense of sin, on the other, resides in the fact that anxiety and guilt are related to one's fellow human beings and a clear sense of sin is related to God. That which our mothers, fathers, brothers, sisters, husband, or wife would consider a very grievous wrong would be easily overlooked by God. That which they would never think of would be foremost in our relationship to God, namely, our prideful unteachableness, our unwillingness to forgive, and our idolatry. The covenant of confession is in relation to God as he is known in Jesus Christ. Here is One who tells us all that we have ever done and yet accepts us, receives us, forgives us. Entry into this covenant of confession activates a deeper resolve in the counselee: a covenant of forgiveness and restitution.

The Covenant of Forgiveness and Restitution. The person

who feels that he has been accepted and forgiven moves to reconsider all the other relationships of his life. The counselee who has faced his own humanity and has been accepted by God is more permissive with those about him. He ceases to expect perfection in others and can make more room for their personal shortcomings. Even though they have committed grievous errors, he can reassess his relationship to them and be more forgiving toward them. The commitment to do this is a covenant of forgiveness for the wounds that one has received. This in turn reminds one of the wounds he has inflicted in the conflict with others. He is likely to discuss with the pastoral counselor at this stage the various things he can do to make restitution and to repair damages he has inflicted. This is a covenant of moral responsibility which reflects the distinctly ethical task of the pastoral counselor. One clinical note from the annals of Alcoholics Anonymous becomes relevant in most counseling relationships that reach this stage of maturity. The Alcoholic Anonymous agrees to make amends to those whom he has harmed, "except where to do so would cause more harm." Thus the covenant of forgiveness and restitution is such as to redeem and not to perpetuate the sufferings arising between people.

The Covenant of Concern. The genuinely profound changes that can and do take place in private pastoral counseling can and do issue in a new covenant of concern on the part of the person or group who has changed and been changed. This is a much more crucial stage of pastoral counseling than is true of other forms of counseling. The professional pastoral counselor who makes his living through individual and group fees, for instance, has a fee-taking structure through which the counselee regularly expresses his concern and gratitude through the fees that he pays. The pastoral counselor who is supported by a church, a school, or some other institution has the resources of the church itself to which to relate the person's concerns for other people and especially for himself as a person. However, the pastor may be so impressed by the superficial changes that have taken place in the reordering of his counselee's life that he will ignore the significance of the counselee's need to express his gratitude. His subtle adoration of the counselor himself may be the way the counselee covenants to make this concern known. For example, Jesus was acutely aware of the Gadarene demoniac's gratitude when the man wanted to go with him wherever he went. Rather, Jesus sent the man back to his own home village as a witness to his recovery. This was probably the most difficult task the man could have been assigned. But Jesus chose to deflect the man's adoration from himself as an individual to the community that needed him desperately, i.e., to the citizens of Gadara, who were busy with the swine!

The Phase of Community Involvement

The person who has profited from pastoral counseling still lives in the same community with the pastor. The private counseling now begins to take on a public quality. His witness to the rest of the community by whatever changes have been affected in his life intimately bespeaks the quality and motivation of the pastor's work. On the other hand, his relationship to the living community of the church becomes crucial. A person who carried a burden of shame and who felt that he was "not fit" to be in a church can now attend with a new sense of joy and participation. The person who vowed that he would never attend church again because of wrongs done him by some other member of the church can now, after having received the concentrated encouragement of the intensive relationships of pastoral counseling, return to church of his own accord. The person who used the church as an atonement procedure by attending every meeting and wanting to run everything can now participate in the life of the church without so much compulsiveness.

Furthermore, the average counseling relationship refocuses in the latter phases of the interview situation. The decisions that have been made and the covenants that have been resolved must be "carried out" in daily living. The couple who were having severe marital difficulties will now begin to be concerned about their children in a way that they previously were not. The young couple who underwent more intensive counseling in their engagement period will need the resources of the church in establishing their home. The older person who is bereaved by the loss of a spouse will need the continuing sustenance of the people his own age in the church. The church provides an avenue both for expressing new concerns and for receiving the concern of others.

In those instances where the process of counseling bogged down or the person refused to make a decision of any kind, the pastor still has the resources of the church to draw upon in ministering to the individual. The person may well be so irresponsible emotionally that medical and psychiatric ministries are indicated. His very illness may be represented by his inability to make decisions and covenants. The pastor may well call upon professional medical resources, but he always does so in the name of the church.

A clear distinction has been made here between pastoral counseling and psychotherapy. The assumption concerning pastoral counseling is that it is done by the pastor of a church, a chaplain in a hospital, or a minister who teaches in a school, etc. In this sense pastoral counseling is one function of the total role of such persons. Only occasionally do these persons do work that approximates the psychotherapeutic relationship, technically defined. Rather, they are involved in a larger public community—a church, a school, or a hospital. These institutions are integral and not incidental to the whole relationship of pastoral counseling. As has been said before, the uniqueness of pastoral counseling emerges at this very point.

The pastor and his counselee are a part of an ongoing community, and the covenant of concern that springs up within the life of the individual is tested and affirmed in his relationships in this community. The most satisfying aspect of pastoral counseling rests in the establishment of the counselee and those about him in the fellowship of faith, concern, and suffering known as the church. Furthermore, the most exacting judgments of the efficacy of pastoral counseling lie in the outcome *within the community* of many so-called successes in individual conferences. Yet, if these judgments seem harsh, the pastor's mistakes are also overruled in the larger wisdom of time and community. What he considered to be failures are later seen to be successes. But the decisive covenants made in pastoral counseling in either instance are carried out in the continuing multifaceted work of the pastor.

PRIVATE COUNSELING AND PUBLIC SOCIAL ACTION

All that has been said focuses upon the private counseling relationship. The objective of such counseling, contrary to protestations of social action critics, is not the mere adjustment of people to the faulty institutions of society. As Don Browning says, effective pastoral care and counseling "acknowledges that it has a larger context which somehow or other governs its specific goals and procedures." He says that pastoral counseling techniques should "reflect and implement" the goals of the church and of the larger culture of society in general. (Don Browning, "Notes on the Context of Pastoral Care," unpublished paper.) Yet, as was indicated in the discussion of the institutional and personal dimensions of pastoral counseling, much that actually goes on in pastoral counseling has come to pass because both church and society are not taking responsibility for the private personal needs of the person that cannot be covered by their own rituals, routines, and over-the-counter panaceas for human suffering. In turn, much is learned in the privacy of the counseling room that gives the pastor a "microscopic lab report" on the massive social injustices that need changing. Such reports make the ethically and socially conscious pastoral counselor much more realistic and less sentimental about *what* social action needs to be taken and *how* to see to it that the changes are actually made.

Consequently, the phase of community involvement in pastoral counseling often turns the counseling relationship into a "coaching relationship" as the counselee battles with changing a defective home situation, a set of working conditions, the interpretation of the role of women, prejudice about race, specific relationships to the poor, precise injustices in the military draft, and severe damage to human life in situations such as mining, the textile industry, and migrant agricultural work. A counseling session may be a time-out from the battle for changes in these situations. Regular infusions of ego strength are needed for such social action battles. Much pastoral counseling today, for example, is with public figures who are change agents. Some pastoral counseling is with power figures who are resisting change. They are in the process of making faulty judgment decisions, or need counseling as a result of some of the threats to their lives.

Several issues arise and certain procedures are necessitated when private pastoral counseling and public social action work hand in glove together. Let me enumerate a few.

Preaching and Pastoral Counseling

The routine public appearance of the minister is as a preacher. Too many pastors are confined to this one medium, but do not need to be. Frederick W. Robertson, the English preacher of the first half of the nineteenth century, was a social activist in the early days of the labor movement. He reserved his sermons for meaty Biblical exegesis in a context of worship. But for debating controversial issues he used lectures in his own church and community. The pastor today could well copy this, because much of the resistance he gets from using the sermon as a tool of social change comes from the injustice people feel because they cannot interrupt him to contradict *or* to reenforce what he is saying. The lecture situation provides just that opportunity. It also provides more time to develop arguments and provide detail.

The *forum* and the *panel* provide the additional force of other voices than that of the pastor as a way of shaping attitudes on social issues. A variety of positions on issues could be implemented. The hard facts of ethical and cultural pluralism in our churches, as well as in our larger community, could be made public. Thus the rigidity of our respectability "front" could be limbered up a bit.

The private pastoral counseling relationships can serve as a "feedback loop," as the communications experts call it, for enabling a pastor to identify *what* issue to discuss in public and to follow up the results of his public discussions. Persons who are deeply affected by such social problems will often come to a public meeting when they would never ask for private help. Massive numbers of people can begin to form a relationship of trust with a pastor through preaching, lecturing, and forums. They can then be helped on an individual, private basis in much less time. Whole families can participate together in these public experiences and then can be provided with private family therapy as a family unit.

The public discussion of issues, however, raises the problem of the specific use of counseling data from private conferences in preaching. Several things can be said about this as concrete guidelines. First, the pastor should plan ahead of time for any such references and not ad-lib about his counseling experiences. This adds reflection to impulse. Second, the preacher should have the person's permission in advance to make such a reference in public. The person could then participate in "the making of the sermon." I have even had people, without my asking, write down for me what they would like said. Then *their* witness is borne in their own words. At least, their permission and approval of a written version of precisely what will be said is only reasonable and right. Third, the pastor should say in public only that which edifies or builds up the person, and should leave unsaid that which would embarrass, hurt, or betray the person. Many uses of case material are little more than horrible examples being held up in contempt. Other uses are expressions of frustration and anger on the part of the preacher. Yet when the person's courage in the face of adversity, humor in the face of life or death, and commitment to God in spite of injustice are told, this becomes "good news," which is what preaching at its best is.

The plight of some of these persons serves as a magnifying glass for the sickness of a community as a whole, for target on social changes that need to be made, etc. This case material can, when finely honed, become parables of modern man, modeled after the parables of Jesus.

Writing and Social Action. The pastor today has the medium of publication as an instrument of social change. He can gather mountains of data from personal counseling attempts to help change social conditions. For example, a mountainous set of problems recur in marriage counseling—problems precipitated by the wife taking a job. In our present inflated economy, the working wife and mother is becoming the rule rather than the exception. A broad-scale approach to the provision of adequate day care for children of parents of all stations in life is a social change that needs to be made. The problems of poverty, race, and family disorganization are all tangled together in this need. The pastor can write for the local newspaper, for the ecclesiastical newspapers, and for the publishing houses of denominations to raise the awareness of people to this need. When he does so he can do something specific about *one* of the objectives of women's liberation. (See Robin Morgan, ed., *Sisterhood Is Powerful*; Random House, Inc., 1970.)

Any topic is "open season" for writing "tracts for the times" in order to effect social change. It is one way of going on record as a citizen on public issues. A reverse kind of private ministry is thus set in motion. Anonymous telephone calls, threats, and underground reactions can occur. At least, I have had it happen periodically.

The Pastor as an Organizer. Social action is so much talk unless specific changes are made in old structures and unless new structures are organized to meet new needs. The tight-knit nuclear family with fixed roles for fixed people in a fixed small-town society still meets the needs of small-town families for a haven of privacy from the extended family of the church and community where everybody knows too much about everybody else. On the other hand, the tight-knit nuclear family in a large city where the neighborhood is also nonexistent is left in isolation and with little or no life-support system. The nuclear family can be and is pulverized by economic aggrandizement of property owners, by the jungle of an impossible school system, and by the spiraling of the costs of food where there are no gardens, pigs and cattle, chickens and fish.

Therefore, the pastor in a large city who sees this happening to family after family is an inadequate pastoral counselor unless he begins to venture with groups of families to meet one another's needs for community, for concerted power to act as families in unison, and to share their unused surpluses in meeting one another's needs. Accordingly, a group of young families renting in the same New York apartment building formed a cooperative for purchasing at quantity and wholesale prices. Another group in the Old Cambridge Baptist Church in Old Cambridge, Massachusetts, began an experiment in cooperative ownership of property as a group of families. This takes time and energy in organizing, and unless a minister is willing to be a part of efforts to change structures more adequately to activate the love of God and neighbor, then his pastoral counseling, like his preaching, fund-raising, and membership recruitment may be parasitic, feeding upon rather than productive of human potentials.

Private Pastoral Counseling as a Form of Social Action

Thomas à Kempis once said that no man can safely appear abroad until he has first disciplined himself to stay out of sight. It does not take a sophisticated person to see that some —not all—of the efforts at social action in the last decade were motivated, in part at least, by the desire for publicity, by the desire for excitement, and by the desire to destroy. When the publicity, the excitement, and the opportunity to vandalize disappeared, a considerable portion of the social activism receded. Yet the social problems remain, although their shapes may have changed. Although young men are no longer under the hammer of the draft, thanks to much social activism, the problems of children in Vietnam are still horrendous at this writing. The urban renewal movement tore down the slums, but the poor still have impossible rents and the elderly are segregated more and more.

The people who make decisions about these inequities are quite often—for other reasons—the counselees of pastors. Many pastors serve as private chaplain to powerful politicians, industrialists, and financiers. As has been nationally observed, outstanding evangelists are being pressed into public identification with political leaders. We know what these ministers do publicly; we wonder what they do privately as counselors to heads of government. Are they captives of the publicity? Are they tools used for political purposes? Do they have any confrontations in private? The answers to these questions are not known.

Historically, the private counseling of power figures by pastors, prophets, and priests has been recorded only anecdotally. Jeremiah was sent for by Zedekiah, the king. "The king questioned him secretly in his house, and said, 'Is there any word from the Lord?' Jeremiah said, 'There is.' Then he said, 'You shall be delivered into the hand of the king of Babylon.'" (Jer. 37:17.) Nathan also counseled with David the king concerning his rebellion against God in having had Uriah the Hittite killed and for having taken the man's wife. (II Sam. 12:1–5.) A curious commentary about the private vs. the public dimensions of life appears in Nathan's words from the Lord to David: "For you did it secretly; but I will do this thing before all Israel, and before the sun." When we overidentify being prophetic with the public activities of a minister, these two quiet conversations in secret with power figures must be remembered. Sometimes the quiet confrontation of a courageous personal counseling interview can effect as much social change as much public, visible protest.

For example, the quiet visit of a pastor in a Southern state, along with three of his lay church members, to the governor of the state concerning the rights of blacks in that whole state did as much to change the structures of discrimination as did much public clamor. One reason was that the three laymen were heavy contributors to the governor's campaign fund. The four of them—the laymen and the pastor together—did not have to raise their voices to convince the governor that it was to *his* advantage to withdraw a certain order. Yet no one received much publicity, not even from the governor, as to why the order was withdrawn.

My hypothesis about the private role of pastors in social action has not, to my knowledge, been researched thoroughly. And the measurable effects of the involvement of pastors in public techniques of social change have not been researched to any great extent, either. The tension between social activist critics of pastoral counseling and the general trends of the movement of pastoral counseling is a healthy one. We stand tempted to be parasitically rather than creatively involved in the established structures of church and society, particularly in the economy. We can become fat and at ease in Zion with little or no social passion or concern. Socially sensitive and ethically aware pastoral counselors, however, have a rebuttal: Our tension with the social action enthusiasts is at two points. (1) There is more than one method of social action, and our life-style is more adaptable to private methods than to public ones, although both have the same objectives. (2) Since we have seen human injustice microscopically in the counseling room, our methods of social action are geared to the pragmatic intention of actually getting results and not just to the satisfaction of having spoken about results and of having been seen trying to get results. At this last point, the sound and fury of much social action effort is just that and it signifies nothing measurable in actual changes.

The Pastor as Politician

The question arises as to the role of the pastor—both public and private—as a political figure. I frankly have had a commitment as a political spirit since my days as a page in the United States Senate. The disturbing thing to me about pastors as politicians is that we tend to become politically concerned only when our own vested interests are at stake. A congregation may think it quite appropriate when a pastor becomes concerned about the taxation of church-owned property, about Sunday closing laws, and—in many instances—about alcoholic beverage control laws. These are self-maintenance concerns. Yet, when a minister becomes politically active about equal housing rights, equal job opportunities for women (and especially black women), about adequate treatment facilities for alcoholics, and about the confusion of four generations of late adolescents by the draft, then he has begun to "mix politics and religion." The most ardent opponents he tends to have are persons who are lawyers. We have worked very hard at relating ourselves as ministers to medical doctors, social workers, and psychologists. The lines between the professional politicians, most of whom are lawyers, however, is a cold war battle line as formidable as the Berlin Wall. Yet these professionals are by profession *counselors*-at-law. The great dividing wall of hostility to be scaled in another era of pastoral counselors is between the professional politicians and ourselves.

The pastoral counselor must recognize that in the matter of being or not being political, he has no choice. By nature, any public office, such as that of pastor, is inherently political in the classical sense of the word. The pastor's choice is between being an ethically consistent and socially effective politician and being a self-serving and/or socially ineffective politician.

The essential correspondence between the pastor as a counselor and the pastor as a politician is that both roles call for a "weight of being." The degree of personal charisma and its attendant power of persuasion that a minister has is increased or decreased in terms of his seniority in a community and the ways in which he has stood by and cared for people in good times and bad times. When he chooses to "throw his weight around" on a given issue, he must "weigh in" first. Even when he decides that he has such power, he is bound to use that power according to the historic—though not necessarily cultural—identity and function of a representative (of the right kind) of God. He cannot fritter it away on trivialities. As John

Henry Newman said, the good confessor must bypass the small things with permissiveness and wait for the emergence of the larger issues of the corporate ethical life. Wherever ministers have been effective as politicians, they have not been squeamish or careless stewards of the power they possess. Nor have they perceived it as *their* power to be used cleverly. Rather, they have used this power on a face-to-face basis; they have used it carefully, as stewards of a gift; they have perceived the power as a gift from God and not of themselves. Yet, withal, they have not permitted a finicky pietism to cause them to disdain the use of power. They have not permitted a covert return of pietism in which they play games about the use of power. (Such a game is played when pastors preserve their pietism by thinking of themselves euphemistically as some sort of "change agents." Thus they avoid thinking of themselves as what they are: politicians.) And, finally, ministers who are effective politicians have learned not to expect utopian success in *every* political effort: they win some, and they lose some! The crucial test of character is whether they can laugh in *both* instances or only when they win.

The ability to laugh as a politician focuses the issue of manipulation by the pastor—or anyone else—as a politician. As Adlai Stevenson said upon losing the race for President: "I am too old to cry, and it hurts too bad to laugh." When he said this, he ruled out another necessary component of manipulation—deception. He was honest. On the other hand Richard Nixon, upon losing the race for the California governorship, announced to newspaper reporters that he was through with politics. While the people were believing him, he laid plans to become President. The issue of manipulation is always at stake when a pastor uses power. Four conditions must prevail: a *conflict of goals* between him and his adversary; an *intention* to cause his adversary to do something the adversary does not want to do; a deliberate *deception* in keeping the person from knowing all that he needs to know to make an informed choice; a *sense of elation, glee, and laughter* at having "outdone," "taken," or "fooled" the adversary. These are, according to Ben

Bursten, the stuff of which manipulation is made. (*The Manipulator*, pp. 95 ff.; Yale University Press, 1973.)

The pastor is a part of a secular and religious culture that "laughs with" a considerable range of manipulators. The great contribution that the psychological disciplines of trained pastoral counselors can provide for the social action efforts of the pastor in discharging his ethical responsibilities is to test his motives for social action by relieving him of his naïveté about changing structures of society and at the same time testing his lust to be clever.

Manipulation, it seems to me, is of four orders: (1) manipulation of the powerful by the powerless out of anger at injustice, in order to survive as persons; (2) manipuation as a mechanical habit formed in a situation where survival was at stake but continued in later situations where manipulation is no longer really necessary; (3) manipulation as a luxury of the clever who manipulate for the sheer delight of reinforcing their self-concept of themselves as omnipotent and all-wise (this is cleverness for cleverness' sake); (4) manipulation as the use of old habits, learned in times of struggle for personal survival, for the purpose of protecting the helpless, providing for the desolate, and introducing the element of fairness in conflicts where the odds are uneven.

Each pastor has to be wiser than the children of darkness, and as wise as a serpent and as harmless as a dove, because he does his work as a sheep in the midst of wolves. Only in his prayers can he decide what kind of manipulator he is.

Chapter 9

THE GROUP
AND THE INDIVIDUAL

The small group is a halfway house between open community involvement and the intensive, one-to-one personal counseling relationship. One of the strategies for relieving some of the tension from the ambiguity between a minister's private work with individuals and his public work with congregations, social structures, and political responsibilities has been the use of small groups for purposes of ministry. A small group is a face-to-face group of persons who are related to one another in what Fritz Kunkel used to call "the We-relationship." They experience a social unity with one another. They know one another, and the membership of their group is relatively constant and clearly defined. The rest of the world, either individuals or masses, is thought of as being distinct from the group.

One could say that there are primary groups such as the family and the school class, spontaneous groups such as a street gang, and socially constructed groups such as a pastor would organize for task-accomplishment purposes, counseling purposes, etc. Ordinarily when we speak of a *small* group, we are speaking of groups that have a maximum of twenty-five people in them. In a study of gangs, for example, Frederic M. Thrasher found that nearly 70 percent of 895 gangs of boys which he had studied had twenty-five or fewer members.

Nearly half had fewer than fifteen members. These were spontaneously generated groups. For purposes of discussion here, we shall think of the small group as being composed of approximately fifteen or fewer members, as having a constant rather than a changing membership, and as having been organized by a trained leader.

The interfaces of such a small group have the mass or the crowd on the one side and the individual as an individual on the other. The multiplex relationships of the pastor involve him in all three of these distinct entities of human interaction. It seems to me that the halfway house between the masses and the individual is, as I have said, the small group. We need to look at the small group, in the first place, in terms of its interaction with the masses; in the second place, in terms of its interaction with individual counseling, and in the third place, in terms of its interaction with itself.

SMALL GROUPS AND THE MINISTRY TO THE MASSES

Historically, a sort of spontaneous combustion has demonstrated that mass movements tend to generate small-group life, which in turn tends to maintain the vitality of the mass movement. Several examples can be cited to illustrate this.

The first of these examples is the Wesleyan revival. Wesley called the world his parish. The class meeting was not superimposed upon his preaching to the masses as a sort of "technique" for carrying on his revival. As Mary Alice Tenney says: "It bore an organic relationship to the ongoing movement, springing spontaneously from the deeply-felt needs of the converts, namely, the sharing of material possessions, the maturing of spiritual life, and the strengthening of the bonds of Christian fellowship." The earliest need that the group met was a financial one. Groups were organized for the purpose of paying off debts on the Methodist chapel room in Bristol, England. The task force was formed and sent out to collect funds. However, on making the calls for funds, the collectors discovered many problems among their class members, such as bereavement, drunkenness, family quarrels. "Religious counseling was added to the duties of the visitors. But soon the task of weekly visitation became too formidable for most of them. It was then that the meeting of classes became a weekly event, where inquiries were made into the spiritual state of each member, problems were freely discussed, and Christian nurture was accomplished." (Samuel Emerick, ed., *Spiritual Renewal for Methodism*, p. 16; Methodist Evangelical Materials, 1958.)

A second example of the reciprocity between mass movements and small groups is found in the Great Awakening revivals which swept from New England through Pennsylvania and Ohio, Kentucky, Tennessee, Arkansas, Oklahoma, and Texas, and into the Eastern seaboard Southern states. Several charges of mass enthusiasm were set off in the eighteenth century by such persons as Jonathan Edwards, George Whitefield, Samuel Davies, and such missionary-minded persons as David Brainerd, Eleazar Wheelock, and Samuel Kirkland. The aftermath of the Great Awakening first took the form of denominational organization into mission societies under what Edwin S. Gaustad calls "denominational generalship." However, the mass revival itself would have spontaneously generated Bible study and Sunday school activity. Out of the larger movement smaller differentiated groups of persons studying the Bible together in Sunday school probably took over, sustained, and refined the more durable aspects of the revival.

Today in some denominations the revival is a sacred institution calculated to gather outsiders into the life of the churches through profession of faith. In practice, the outsiders are not gathered into the fellowship of faith nearly as often as persons who have already been participants in small-group activities such as Sunday school classes, choirs, and youth fellowships. These small groups have, in effect, taken over the function of the mass revival, which is, however, held as a sort of festival and as a way of timing the formal recognition that members of these small groups are indeed also members of the larger congregation.

A third example of reciprocity between small groups and the masses is the contemporary revival phenomenon of such persons as Billy Graham and Oral Roberts. One of the most vital aspects, for example, of the Billy Graham crusades is the way in which the advance workers come into a community and establish a vast network of small groups at the neighborhood level. They gather at stated times in order to listen to radio messages, tapes, etc., by Graham himself. These in turn serve as a basis for discussion, fellowship, preparation, and self-examination.

A fourth example of the interaction between the mass approach to people's problems and the small-group approach, strangely enough, was effected in 1930 by a psychiatrist named L. C. Marsh. He applied certain techniques in a large state hospital. (L. C. Marsh, "Group Treatment of the Psychoses by the Psychological Equivalent of the Revival," *Mental Hygiene*, Vol. XV, 1931, pp. 328–340.) J. W. Klapman says that Marsh's first large-scale therapy was borrowed from the practices of organized religion, from Rotary, and from teaching techniques. Marsh created a festive air with as many as five hundred patients attending at a time. His chief objective was to stimulate intellectually and emotionally persons who had lost this sense of feeling. He used the crowd to "bring their emotional interest into squad formation, to discipline and direct them toward life." (J. W. Klapman, *Group Psychotherapy: Theory and Practice*, 2d ed., p. 7; Grune & Stratton, Inc., 1959.) Other psychiatrists, such as Louis Wender, were attracted to Marsh's imaginative ideas but moved in the direction of smaller groups. The organization Recovery is an outgrowth of Dr. A. A. Low's group therapy at Illinois Neuro-Psychiatric Institute. Through study groups and house parties patients continue group relationship during post-hospitalization. Here again, a mass effort at reaching large numbers of people with help tended to catalyze into small-group formations.

Many other examples of the reciprocal dynamism working between mass movements and small-group formations could be cited at the religious and therapeutic level as well as at the political and economic level. However, these examples suffice to demonstrate that small groups are no new invention; they tend to form spontaneously if they are not guided into formation. They seem to be here to stay in one form or another.

SMALL GROUPS AND INDIVIDUAL COUNSELING

The individual counseling ministry of the pastor stands over against the other interface of small-group relationships. If a pastor takes seriously individual counseling of a more intense kind, he will tend quite naturally to move in the direction of small-group formations as a result of his counseling. As he forms small-group sessions with selected people, he will also find that individuals within these groups will draw upon his time for a variety of reasons that are dynamically related to what goes on in the group. Either he or someone else on a planned or spontaneous basis will still face the responsibility of dealing with the individual needs of the person. The second portion of this chapter is calculated to clarify the reciprocity between and the inseparability of individual and group counseling. Enthusiasm for either individual or group counseling can obscure this reciprocity and inseparability of the two forms of assistance to people.

Repetitive Problems of Individual Counseling

The pastor who does much individual counseling soon discovers in any environment that a large number of the problems that people present are similar, if not the same. For example, a pastoral counselor in a theological seminary where 70 percent of the students are married will repetitively face the problem of isolation of the student from his wife and vice versa. The pastor in any setting will meet repeatedly persons who are bereaved. In a time of spiraling inflation, money problems will begin to take a repetitive and monotonous form. Individual counseling is considerably limited in that it keeps these people from sharing with each other the fruits of their own experience in solving the particular problems they face.

Individual counseling maintains their isolation with the problem. They are likely to assume that they are the only ones who have such problems.

The constant repetition of the same kinds of problems wears on the patience of the individual counselor and is likely to push him into the corner of prepackaged answers. Impatience may obscure some of the issues of the person's life deeper than the particular problem itself. The pastor may also be tempted to throw away all that he has learned and to start lecturing, preaching, or exhorting—whichever happens to be his way of doing all the talking.

However, in a group, the pastor and the counselee discover, as Harry Stack Sullivan has said, that we are more distinctly human than otherwise. We have far more in common than whatever separates us from each other. Also, as the apostle Paul says, "No temptation has overtaken you that is not common to man." (I Cor. 10:13.) Even the experience of confession can, in and of itself, often be done on a group basis with as much or more effect than when it is done on an individual basis. As the pragmatic spirit of the book of James indicates: "Confess your sins to one another, and pray for one another, that you may be healed." (James 5:16.) Joseph W. Knowles says, "The counseling group in the church context provides a new wineskin through which to restore the confessional ministry and enable the church to become the confessional community." (*Group Counseling*, p. 33; Prentice-Hall, Inc., 1964.) The limitation of individual counseling in facing repetitive problems such as has been mentioned here is a distinct limitation of the experience of any one person to be able to empathize with all people. In a group setting the span of empathy possibility is widened.

Pathology vs. Growth

Historically, individual counseling done by pastors has grown up in close proximity to sick people and to professional persons who have a "pathology model" for viewing and helping people. Illness tends to isolate, individualize, and accent the idiosyncrasies of people. Howard Clinebell told me that, in his opinion, the more one moves away from the pathology model and toward the human potential and growth model of the positive resources of persons for meeting life and planning for its defeats and successes, the more one moves away from individual counseling as the sole method of care and moves toward a group approach to counseling. Upon further reflection since he made this comment, I do not think that he meant to infer that the reverse of this point of view is true, namely, that the more nearly sick a person is, the less valuable to him are group procedures. Such a point of view would nullify a vast body of data collected in psychoanalytic approaches to groups such as those of Slavson, Yalom, and others. I prefer to use the term "group therapy" to identify that specific kind of group treatment and group work being done with persons in a hospital environment or as outpatients who have identifiable clinical syndromes of function-interfering and crippling illness. I also reserve the term "group therapy" for doctors and other hospital-related personnel.

One relationship between individual counseling and group counseling is that of the individual screening of persons who are being permitted to enter the group. Such screening helps to identify real pathological entities. Some sort of evaluative interview on an individual basis, it seems to me, is ordinarily indicated. Many groups, however, are formed *in toto* from the outset without such individual screening procedures. This is, in my opinion, a strategic mistake. Manifestly the purpose of these individual screening procedures would be to identify insofar as is possible those persons who lack a readiness for group counseling. My hypothesis is that there are many people who are ready for individual counseling who are not necessarily ready for group counseling. Conversely, many people are ready for group counseling who are not yet prepared to deal with a pastoral counselor or any other kind of counselor on an intensely individual basis.

Implicit within the assertions that I have just made is a basic point of view which I have adopted from András Angyal. He, being a psychiatrist, has set forth the point of view which he calls "the theory of universal ambiguity." Angyal says, "Everything in life has a double meaning, hence universal ambiguity." He rejects the idea of "sickness" as being the "rotten part of a healthy apple." He also rejects the idea that "health" is a segregated part or hidden region of a personality. On the contrary, both health and pathology are present throughout the whole personality. "Health is present potentially in its full power and so is the most destructive, most baneful, most shameful behavior." Likewise, pathology rests in its full potential in the most altruistic, most admirable, and most productive behavior. There is a "dual patterning of personality." Shifts of dominance take place from time to time in the same individual. These shifts may be dramatic or they may be gradual. The most striking example, probably, is that of a neurotic impulse being made to serve health by making a suicidal attempt turn out to be a plea for help. (András Angyal, *Neuroses and Treatment: A Holistic Theory*, pp. 102–111; John Wiley & Sons, Inc., 1965.)

Therefore, individual and group counseling can be placed on a continuum that is correlative with a continuum between pathology and health. The ambiguity that lies along both continua, however, keeps me from settling the tension on either end of the two continua. Furthermore, training and experience in *both* individual counseling and group counseling are necessary for adequate pastoral counseling. The pastoral counselor who has not "clocked in" intensive amounts of time in individual counseling and in dealing with seriously disturbed people even of psychotic proportions is poorly prepared. He is only dimly aware of the complexity of the ambiguity between the concepts called "illness" and "health." Nevertheless, coming from a leader such as Howard Clinebell, who has indeed done his fair share of work with severely disturbed people on an individual basis, such a rough generalization as he has made is to me an unusually helpful one. The more a person works with relatively healthy people, the more he finds group procedures to be the tools of choice. The more he works with acutely disturbed people, the more nearly individual counseling meets their need.

The Need for Life-Support Systems

Pastoral counselors, social workers, psychologists, psychiatrists, and psychoanalysts have a colloquial way of saying that we are "carrying" a certain number of counselees, clients, or patients. This implies that they are a "load." It implies more literally that we are "holding them up." In more recent technical terminology, one might say that the individual counselor or therapist has become the counselees' or the patients' "life-support system." The counselor has become a "bridge over troubled waters" for these persons. He holds them up. Otherwise they might be submerged in the abyss of meaninglessness and purposelessness of life. Immediately the reader could rightly ask: "What do you mean by a life-support system?"

A person's life-support system is that group of people who are both nourishing and realistic in their relationship to him. They are that group of people whom one trusts and can be intimate and honest with, free of gamesmanship. They are that group of people who relate to one meaningfully; they do not use one as a tool for their own purposes. A person's life-support system is composed of people who are warm and caring in a nonpossessive way. They are persons who are genuine and without shame. But, most of all, they are people who won't desert or abandon one. An individual counselor, whether he sees the person occasionally, often, or seldom, can indeed be a life support to his counselee.

However, a group of people led by the same counselor multiply the number of foci of energy in the support system of a person. Not only do they provide support for that individual, they also give that person the opportunity to provide support for them. The member of a group can learn not only to be ministered unto but also to minister. As such, the group relationship has something to offer in the way of a life-support system which is highly limited in individual counseling.

Peer Group Involvement and Reality Testing

Another limitation of individual counseling is that only a given set of feelings or ideas or behaviors can be explored psychologically. They can be tested to a limited degree by the individual reactions of the counselor. This is a distinct limitation in that one man's opinion is not a very wide range for reality-testing. Furthermore, the individual counselee, in testing some of his more negative feelings with his counselor, is often overwhelmed by the counselor. In group counseling, the peer group challenges the unrealism of some of the thinking of the individual; at the same time the group provides comradeship when the individual decides to express negative feelings toward the leader. In this sense the group leader also has an opportunity to test his own perception of his counselee by that of other people in the group. Thus his impression has the possibility of being more just and accurate.

In the peer group situation the sibling problem is activated. In individual counseling the counselee is for all practical purposes "an only child" in the elements of transference that occur in the relationship. In a peer group, however, the "only child" syndrome is overcome; the individual has to relate himself to the other members of the group as well as to the leader. If he is desperately in need of socialization, this is an opportunity for him to try his wings at it. In my own clinical practice, I often work for a period of time with an individual on a one-to-one basis until I sense that he is beginning to reach out to find other people. When this happens and the shell of social isolation is broken, I tend to involve the person in a group experience. The group can do things for him that no amount of individual attention can provide.

The Time Factor in Individual Counseling

Individual counseling is an extremely time-consuming process. This is one reason why a considerable number of pastors never make a second appointment to talk with a given counselee. They try to deal with everyone on a one-interview basis.

They perceive themselves to be too pressed for time to provide more than one interview. More disciplined and thoroughgoing pastoral counselors often find that some counselees will keep coming back on a one-interview basis again and again and again. Time could be saved if a process of counseling could be developed with them. Even more time can be saved and more people can be reached if one spends an hour and a half with —let us say—ten people than if one spends an hour with one person. This rationale for group counseling has been played back often in the literature on the subject. But time-saving is the least convincing of the reasons for having group counseling as over against individual counseling. The person may or may not need a group as well as time. Nevertheless, time being as limited as it is, this argument is an important one in behalf of group counseling as opposed to individual counseling.

The Creative Use of Energy

Individual counseling, when properly done, is an energy-consuming and taxing experience. This is true both for the counselee and for the counselor. The relationship tends to be more distinctly problem- and pathology-oriented and the drain on the energies of counselor and counselee is greater when moments of celebration, affirmation, and rejoicing are less frequent than they are in a group situation. Group members also take some of the pressure of leadership off the counselor, and he can "catch his breath" as they become involved with one another. One reason that a considerable number of people lean more toward group counseling than toward individual counseling seems to be that group work simply tends to be more fun. Often, in individual counseling, a counselee will complain that the counselor knows only his "bad points" and can only assume that there are other "sides" to his nature than the ones he reveals. In group situations the "other sides" tend to express themselves in surprising ways as contrasted with the individual counseling situation. When this happens the energies of both the counselee and the counselor are replenished in a way that is refreshing.

The Financial Cost and Income in Group Counseling

For that sector of pastoral counselors who do charge fees for their services, the factor of cost to the counselee and income for the counselor is a considerable one. Group therapy can be provided for an individual who is a member of a group of ten people at a third or a fourth of what it would cost for individual counseling. On the other hand, the use of the time is more lucrative for the counselor without his feeling that he is "fleecing" his group members. These are quite legitimate objectives for both counselees and counselors where the counselor has put in heavy amounts of time in preparing for his task as a counselor and has become an experienced and wise person, over and above his own supervised clinical education. Money, nevertheless, can be a distorting objective for the poorly trained or the well-trained group leader who finds that group work is a shortcut to a quick dollar. The heavy discipline required of him in being a counselor on a one-to-one basis as a genuine preparation for being a group counselor is easily avoided. One-to-one work with individuals, in my opinion at least, is an imperative necessity in the equipment of an adequate group leader. This position puts me out of step with the more faddistic forms of group counseling which are somewhat rampant in the country today. The love of money is the root of all evil, not the money itself. Both individual counselors and group counselors are subject to the kinds of distortions of motivation that the preoccupation with money can bring into any relationship. One of my concerns is the way in which rather steep costs for group work are appearing over the country. These costs tend to nullify the strength of group counseling as a procedure of choice over individual counseling.

GROUP COUNSELING AS DONE BY PASTORS

The last portion of this chapter examines the distinctly pastoral responsibility and function of group counseling. Pastoral group counseling is extensive today, but the distinctly pastoral dimensions of the counseling have been obscured by the extreme popularity of a wide variety of group-counseling and group-therapy theories and techniques. Many pastoral counselors move from one kind of theory and technique of group counseling to another with little or no pastoral judgment and analysis. Several tributaries of technique and theory can be identified as being exceptionally influential on the process and methodologies of pastors today. A clearheaded discussion of the distinctly pastoral dimensions of group counseling in the contemporary setting cannot be articulated without some explanation of what these tributaries are.

Behavior-Modification Approaches to Group Counseling

Behavior-modification approaches to both individual and group counseling have been derived from learning-theory approaches to personality. The behavioral-group counselor takes a very systematic approach to the group. He leaves no lack of clarity as to what is expected of each group member, although the group member is required to participate in defining the kind of person he hopes to become in the process of group counseling. The individual needs of separate persons in the group are fulfilled by the behavioral-modification counselor meeting with each member in advance of the group meeting. In these individual conferences an agreement is reached as to the behavioral goals of each person. When the group comes together, the job of counselor is to synchronize, synthesize, and mobilize these various goals toward a common purpose of the larger group. The central hypothesis of positive and negative reinforcement of different kinds of behaviors is important in behavioral group counseling. As one can readily see, the behavioral-modification approach to group counseling is an intensively leader-centered kind of group. Furthermore, the counselor concentrates on behavior rather than on fantasies, feelings, faults, etc. (Don C. Dinkmeyer and James J. Muro, *Group Counseling: Theory and Practice,* pp. 54–57; F. E. Peacock Publishers, Inc., 1971.)

Transactional Groups

Eric Berne, in his book *Principles of Group Treatment* (Oxford University Press, Inc., 1966), sets forth the transactional theory of groups. He bases his work upon determining which ego state—Parent, Adult, or Child—is active at a particular time in the transactions between members of the group. They are concerned, and the transactional-group counselor is concerned, with the activity of ego states in sending messages and in responding to messages. He takes an active, directed role, always seeking to hold on to his own Adult functions.

One of the exceptionally valuable parts of transactional approaches to group counseling is the formation of contracts. These contracts seem to me to be of two orders: First, the contract of the leader with each member of the group. Transactional-group leaders tend to have at least one private interview session with each person before he enters the group. A part of this contract upon entering the group also involves the "permission" of the other members of the group in relation to the membership of the new person. The group leader is the negotiator of this contract. Second, contracts appear within the process of each group meeting. Each member of the group is asked what it is that he wants to work on during this session. Contracts that are very attainable within the time limits are stated in the presence of the other members of the group.

Transactional-group counseling focuses upon the clarification of the purposes of the meeting, the establishment of good contracts, the confrontation of individuals with what is happening now in the living present, the identification of various ego states, the clarification of deliberate vagueness on the part of the group member, concentration upon what the person is feeling right now, focus upon what he wants to do about those feelings now. He is responsible for his own feelings and behavior. As Don C. Dinkmeyer and James J. Muro say, "The goal of transactional analysis is to help the individual toward awareness of what is going on in other persons so that he can become completely open and spontaneous, more comfortable, and hence more intimate with his fellow man" (*op. cit.*, p. 59). The advanced transactional group works with each individual and facilitates his awareness of his scripts. "Script" is the name for the long-term, more or less unconscious programmed plan of the life-style of the person.

Group-centered Counseling

Group-centered counseling is more technically known as phenomenological group counseling, having its philosophical origins in the writings of Otto Rank, Jesse Taft, Carl Rogers, Arthur Combs, and Donald Snygg. The phenomenological approach is concerned with the exact nature of an individual's perceptions of himself as he sees himself from within himself. The group leader is a facilitator of the changes that individual members can make in their own behavior and can encourage in one another. These changes come from modifications of the individual's perceptions of himself as a certain kind of self that is acceptable, or unacceptable, etc. In essence group-centered counseling works hard upon the patterning effect of the individual's self-image upon behavior. The reality testing of that perception of one's own self by the responses of other members of his group is one of the purposes of the group. The group-centered counselor emphasizes the process of growth and the perception of the self-image. The assumption is that behavior will change when the self-image changes. The group leader actually functions as an alter ego type member of the group. He models ways which group members can imitate and identify with as they seek to develop their positive strengths as persons.

Training Group and Sensitivity Approaches to Group Counseling

The National Training Laboratories of Bethel, Maine, have established a highly systematized approach to an informal learning kind of group counseling. Their earlier points of view are elaborately set forth in the book entitled *T-Group Theory and Laboratory Method: Innovation and Re-Education* (ed. by Leland P. Bradford, Jack R. Gibb, and Kenneth Benne; John Wiley & Sons, Inc., 1964). The focus of this method of group learning is upon what they call "here-and-now" learning. Instead of concentrating on specific tasks such as becoming a better parent, learning how to counsel others, the group focuses upon the immediate experience of the group members with each other and the leader. As Benne, Bradford, and Gibb say: "The aim of those in charge of laboratory learning is to help the learning group identify and manage (the withholding or distortional responses by persons with whom another person has tried to interact) in such a way that withholding and distortion are reduced and feedback becomes more instantaneous and authentic." (*Ibid.*, p. 25.) Another aim is that of helping people to explore their value commitments openly in a group through public examination and personal reconstruction.

The training-group theory has had extensive influence upon the work of the National Council of Churches and its constituent members as well as upon business organizations whose representatives also tend to "connect up" with these methods as they are used in their churches. In the main, it has been an upper-middle-class and a lower-upper-class operation and has had only minimal relationship to lower classes of the social class system set forth by W. Lloyd Warner in his book *Social Class in America* (Yale University Press, 1960).

The more recent form of laboratory method in group work has taken the form of sensitivity training. The sensitivity group focuses on "giving and receiving feedback" between the members of the group and their facilitator. This method is an effort to construct a "therapy for normals" that emphasizes growth rather than pathology, the present kinds of interaction rather than the past memories, and the existential rather than the didactic modes of learning. The leader does not promote transference reaction, although he is aware that these reactions do happen. (Leonard Horowitz, "Transference in Training

Groups and Therapy Groups," in *Sensitivity Training and the Laboratory Approach,* ed. by Robert T. Golembiewski and Arthur Blumberg, pp. 180–182; F. E. Peacock Publishers, Inc., 1970.)

The sensitivity trainer's goal with his group is the development of the members' awareness of themselves, of others, of group processes, and of group cultures. The movement has enlarged its goals to that of the expansion of consciousness without the use of drugs—consciousness of one's own being, one's own potential, and the sources of joy and intimacy. The work of William Schutz, in his book *Joy* (Grove Press, Inc., 1967), details basic techniques for doing this, such as the release of grief through imaginary conversation with the "lost persons" in the lives of group members, the search for realization of despaired-of goals through "guided fantasies."

Golembiewski points out the limitations of this approach, at the same time he says that many in the movement claim "its always-and-everywhere applicability." He says that *cultural preparedness* is necessary for the use of the methods. Also, the laboratory method of sensitivity is only one of a family of approaches to change in persons and in organizations. He lists six other approaches, for example, in changing organizations: an authority person "decrees" change for lesser authorities, one or more officials leave and are replaced by others, structural reorganizations *may* help individuals function better, group-decision approaches can be used, data-discussion approaches can effect changes, and problem-solving group approaches can be used. He says that there is no single "magic bullet." Third, change agents may intervene to change groups and organizations in ways that do not always require or use the laboratory approach. Golembiewski identifies, with the help of Blake and Moulton, at least nine different kinds of intervention calculated to change groups and structures.

1. *Discrepancy:* by calling attention to contradiction in policy, in attitudes, and in behavior.

2. *Research:* by using research data to expose changes that need to be made.

3. *Procedural critique:* by testing existing procedures.

4. *Experimentation:* by searching out and proposing alternative policies before settling on or maintaining one.

5. *Relationships:* by seeking the improvement of communication and trust between individuals and subgroups.

6. *Dilemmas:* by posing dilemmas for problem-solving;

7. *Perspective:* by recall of historical or situational data and understanding.

8. *Structural critique:* by identifying trouble as inhering in structures and not just in individuals.

9. *Culture:* an appeal to and focus upon tradition and heritage as well as upon norms from the culture itself.

Whereas the sensitivity lab can use some of these approaches, it is "nowhere indispensable nor even necessarily useful." (Robert T. Golembiewski, "Planned Organizational Change," in Golembiewski and Blumberg, eds., *op. cit.*, pp. 365–368.) When pastors become victims of too much enthusiasm for sensitivity training or any other particular models of group and structural change, these guidelines from the most thorough analysis of sensitivity training should be used to abate overzealousness.

Psychoanalytic Approaches to Group Therapy

The hidden agenda in much of the theory presented thus far is the way in which psychoanalytic approaches to groups are implicit in the methods—as in the case of transactional analysis. Or the method may be a studied effort to be different from psychoanalysis, as in the case of behavior modification.

The psychoanalytic group is unique in that it is distinctly a therapeutic group. The therapist assumes that there are neurotic and psychotic possibilities and realities in the group members. He consciously uses the transference and the countertransference as a means of interpreting parental authority and sibling relationships. Longer-term, insight-producing objectives characterize the psychoanalytic group.

Another unique factor in psychoanalytic group therapy is the training of the therapist. Ordinarily the therapist is a certified psychoanalyst or psychiatrist, although a considerable number of clinical psychologists and pastoral counselors, trained in the 1950's and 1960's, also use psychoanalytic assumptions and methods. The model of psychoanalytic group therapy is a pathology model rather than a growth model. Some pastoral counselors rely heavily on the psychoanalytic model and intersperse the group procedure with techniques learned from several of the other patterns for group counseling.

One also observes a swerve in the objectives of other group-counseling approaches in the direction of psychoanalytic assumptions. Not the least of these is that the longer a "facilitator," a "trainer," or a group leader stays in touch with a given group, the more likely he is to do two things: first, to discover the irrational behavior and mentation of which psychoanalysts speak; and, second, to feel the need for more profound and systematic training.

Yet, much of the more recent emphasis on group counseling is studied effort to shorten the group process, to deal with issues of interaction on a "marathon" crash basis, and to disallow the tyranny of the past history as an avoidance of responsibility. My own estimate is that a subterranean reciprocity is taking place between psychoanalysis and the other approaches to group counseling. The real hazard of the psychoanalytic approach is the neglect of "the many" who need therapy less than they need genuine nourishment and direction in growth for the "few" who are fortunate enough—sick or well —to have the money and leisure for long-term therapy. The real hazard of the more recent approaches to group counseling such as behavioral modification, transactional analysis, reality therapy, and others is that the leaders of such groups are really not disciplined in or aware of the problems of differential diagnosis of disease. Not everyone is sick; only one out of ten, let us guess. Even with this ratio, however, the *one* that is sick *could* be *any* one of the members of the group. The burden of responsibility, it seems to me, is on the leader of the group. Outside consultation of physicians of internal medicine, gynecology, psychiatry, and physical medicine can be sought by the leader himself and through referral. Consultation and referral are no substitutes, though, for the leader himself having spent months of discipline in a psychiatric hospital trying to understand "collapsed" persons, and additional months of discipline in a medical center learning the basics of the physiology and disease, the death and dying of the human organism. Group counseling is no different from individual counseling in these demands upon the counselor. There is no substitute for supervised exposure over a period of at least a year and preferably three years that will include intensive research in the crucial human situations to which the human flesh is heir now as always.

Yet, from a pastoral counseling point of view, much leadership of groups in vogue at the time of this writing is superficial and insecure at the point of both the training and the wisdom of the leader. Considerable overdependence upon "exercises" seems to be a cut-flower kind of "pretty gimmick" use that does not continue in fruitful meaning. Pastors, because of their ministerial immunity in the public eye, their uneven acceptance by other professions, and the lack of state and federal laws governing their certification, are particularly vulnerable to crash programs in transactional analysis, behavior modification, sensitivity training, reality therapy, Gestalt therapy, etc. Enthusiasts for such programs often pay high fees for quick results and certification as group process. Yet the crash program trainers themselves often lack the kind of long-term discipline which Eric Berne, William Glasser, and others used as background for their innovations.

Gestalt Therapy Groups

Popularity has come to Gestalt therapy only recently. Well before 1950, persons such as Frederick Perls, Ralph Hefferline, and Paul Goodman were developing a therapeutic modality for the hard-earned gains of Wertheimer, Kohler, and Lewin. They published their approach to therapy in their book, *Gestalt*

Therapy: Excitement and Growth in the Human Personality
(The Julian Press, Inc., 1951). They shifted the emphasis from
the psychoanalytic concern with the unconscious to a systematic approach to *awareness*. Awareness, when it is adequately
functioning, operates in the realms of health, stimulation, and
growth. The characteristics of awareness are *contact, sensing,
excitement,* and *Gestalt formation*. The Gestalt therapist asks
such questions as: "With what and with whom are you in contact?" "What is each of your senses sensing now?" "What phys-
iologically, psychologically, and socially excites you?" "How
do you put things together into totalities, wholes, i.e., Gestalts?"

These questions would have been somewhat esoteric twenty
years ago. Today, however, they are the central concerns of the
counter culture and the persistent interest of many people in
the late 1960's and the early 1970's with the "raising of awareness" or the "expansion of consciousness." The Gestaltists see
the constriction of awareness as the refusal of many people to
feel the disgust that they have incorporated into their own personalities. They are filled with self-loathing to which they can
be insensitive by projecting these feelings onto others. One of
their procedures in group therapy is to have one member of
the group "project" or "lay on" his feelings toward another
member of the group. When he has finished this he is asked
to say the same thing about himself and to "see" how it "feels"
on him. This procedure is calculated to increase awareness of
one's introjections by starting first with projections. These introjections are undigested residues of "forced feeding, forced
education, forced morality, forced identifications with parents
and siblings." They are "unassimilated odds and ends—lodged
in the being of a person." A process of regurgitation of "swal-
lowed" experiences goes on in group therapy. (*Ibid.*, p. 202.)
These are reassimilated and reoriented in acceptable perception.

Much more can be said about each of these theoretical
approaches to groups. Enough has been said, however, to suggest to the reader some directions to take for more detailed
study of the various approaches. All these approaches should

be examined closely for the common elements they share and the uniqueness they offer. Furthermore, enough has been said about them here to show how easy it is to become engrossed in any one or several of them to the exclusion of asking primary pastoral questions or making serious pastoral explorations of their theological relevance, if any.

Some valuable perspectives of various approaches to groups have recently appeared. Irvin Yalom and Morton Lieberman did a confirmatory study of encounter-group casualties. They concluded that there *were* casualties and that previous reports of almost-perfect results were unfounded. They concluded that the particular ideological schools of the leaders, whether psychoanalytic Gestalt, transactional analysis, etc., were unrelated to one another and that, for example, "two transactional analysis leaders were no more likely to resemble one another than they were to resemble leaders from any of the other schools." On the contrary, a taxonomy of leaders had to be developed that had nothing to do with "schools," as such. Two indices were chosen: (1) the symbolic value of the leader to each member and (2) the use of observers to identify leader behavior such as emotional stimulation, caring, meaning, and executive functions. These four functions accounted for 70 percent of leader behavior.

On the basis of these variables, seven types of leaders were identified.

1. *Aggressive Stimulators*. These leaders were characterized by their high-stimulus input. "They were intrusive, confrontive, challenging, while at the same time demonstrating high positive caring; they revealed a great deal of themselves."

2. *"Love Leaders."* These leaders were enlightened paternalists who enabled people to learn at their own pace but did not press.

3. *Social Engineer Leaders*. These leaders majored on steering the group as a whole rather than upon individual and interpersonal dynamics. Little stimulation or confrontation took place. They were distant, cool, and offered little support.

4. *Laissez Faire Leaders*. These leaders seemingly were "just

there"—passive, little stimulation input, no challenging, no confrontation, no support, no structure.

5. *"Cool, Aggressive Stimulators."* These leaders offered little except stimulation, focusing upon group process.

6. *High Structure.* These leaders were highly controlling, authoritarian, and ritualized leaders. They had many "group games" and structured exercises for the group to "go through their paces."

7. *The Tape Leaders.* The Peer Program of Bell and Howell was used in two groups. These tapes provided an essentially leaderless group that concentrated on giving and receiving feedback, making emotional contact with others, and learning to self-disclose. The tapes deemphasized interpersonal conflict.

As to the amount of harm done by these different kinds of leaders, the aggressive stimulators produced the most casualties (44 percent). They not only produced more casualties, but the casualties were more severe. The "tape leaders" in the Bell and Howell recordings produced no casualties.

Yalom and Lieberman isolated the causes of casualties as: (1) attack by the leader or by the group, (2) rejection by the leader or by the group, (3) failure to attain unrealistic goals, (4) "input overloads," and (5) group-pressure effects. (Irvin Yalom and Morton Lieberman, "A Study of Encounter Group Casualties," *Archives of General Psychiatry*, Vol. 25, No. 1, July 1971. See also Morton A. Lieberman, Irvin D. Yalom, and Matthew B. Miles, *Encounter Groups: First Facts*, pp. 425–427; Basic Books, Inc., 1973.)

Three conclusions can be drawn from these findings: (1) Any method of counseling is just as dangerous as it is useful. (2) The amount of damage done varies, not according to the particular theory to which a leader is devoted but to the self-appraising judgment of the leader in offsetting damaging side effects of his treatment. (3) The responsibility for casualties seems to be that of the leader who accepts responsibility for the group members as individuals as well as for the group as a whole whether he admits it or not. It seems to me that leaders' casualty rate depends rather heavily upon whether they become unduly preoccupied with individual or group goals to the exclusion of one or the other.

DISTINCTLY PASTORAL APPROACHES TO GROUPS

The tributaries that we have been exploring flow into the mainstream of an explicitly pastoral approach to group counseling. They may flow into this mainstream, but as they do so they take a new form and a new direction. This point of view can be illustrated as different kinds of pastoral groups are discussed.

The Task-oriented Group

Religious groups have tasks to perform as did Wesley's groups that formed to raise money to pay for the chapel at Bristol. These groups develop additional tasks, such as the care of the bereaved, the alcoholic, the problem family. The focus of the group is external ministry. Nevertheless, group dynamics of power struggle for leadership, competition for the leader's attention and time, and the transference of old "dated emotions" come into play as the group works together. From this angle of vision, the psychoanalytic input flows in to enrich the pastor's understanding of his group members' interaction in "getting the job done." If the members of a group get into conflict with one another, they will begin to "project" upon one another. The pastor, however, would have at his disposal Gal. 6:1–10 as a basis of interpreting the spiritual life: If a man is overtaken in a fault, we restore him gently, and look to ourselves, lest we too be tempted by the same kinds of temptations. Yet, the main job of the task-oriented group is to get the task done—whatever was agreed upon to do.

The "Special Needs" Group

The pastor as an individual counselor meets some perennial special needs of people. High school seniors in the spring are under stress about going to college, staying out of school and working, deciding what to do in relation to their boyfriend or girl friend, etc. They are often in rebellion against their parents' restrictions, in confusion about right and wrong, and feel estranged from their childhood religion.

A group called "a seekers group" can be formed out of the high school seniors in the church. They can enable one another, draw strength from their peer relationships, and have an adult other than their parents with whom to test reality. Old undigested religious "introjects" can be brought up and reexamined. Their struggle between Child ego states and Adult ego states can be plotted on a transactional analysis format. The whole meaning of "lowering the importance of the earthly family" and "gaining access to the larger family of mankind" through faith in God can be a basis for spiritual conversation in the group.

Another need that appears perennially is that for premarital guidance and counseling. Much of this is better done on a group basis, where social groupings can be started early and transitions to a "fellowship of the married" can be made. Howard Clinebell says: "Churches have a major role to play in providing premarital groups, since clergymen perform millions of weddings each year. Groups should be scheduled and publicized at least three or four times a year. Interchurch groups are a possibility if individual churches do not have enough weddings to warrant even occasional groups." (*The People Dynamic*, pp. 91–92; Harper & Row, Publishers, Inc., 1972.)

Other special needs groups can be formed, such as grief therapy groups, divorcées groups, financial planning groups. Special groups such as newlyweds, parents groups, middle-aged-"empty-nest" groups, planning for retirement groups, can be formed. Clinebell's study of groups in his *The People Dynamic* is a storehouse of help for a pastor in forming such groups.

Spiritual Conversation Groups

Much of the discussion of God, of Christ, of the Holy Spirit, of prayer, and of one's own spiritual autobiography and heritage is politely and superficially deleted from both daily life and conversation. Spiritual loneliness and vacuums are the result. People are accustomed to "listening while the minister expounds" on these subjects. He gets little opportunity to listen to the people, and even less to listen to them share with one another on these matters.

One instrument of conversation is the religious history or spiritual autobiography. Edgar Draper has devised the religious ideation questionnaire as a brief tool for catalyzing either individual or group. Dan McKeever made certain additions of his own and provides the following as a useful tool in groups of spiritual conversationalists:

Religious Ideation Questionnaire

1. What is your earliest memory of a religious experience or belief?
2. What is your most significant religious memory?
3. Where did you live from age 1 to 15? Was your environment rural or urban?
4. Did your parents take you to church?
5. How would you describe their religious teachings and training?
6. What kind and amount of religious experience? (Nominal, occasional, regular)
7. When was conversion? What did it mean?
8. Do both you and your husband/wife go to church?
9. Did either of you change churches?
10. Do you take the children? If not, why?
11. Do you participate in church life now? In what way?
12. What is your favorite Bible story?
13. What is your favorite Bible verse?
14. Who is your favorite Bible character?
15. What does prayer mean to you? If you pray, what do you pray for?
16. What does religion mean to you?
17. How would you describe God?
18. How does God function in your personal life?
19. In what way is God meaningful to other people besides yourself?

20. How is God meaningful to your mother or father?
21. What religious idea or concept is most important to you now?
22. What is the most religious act one can perform?
23. What do you consider the greatest sin one could commit?
24. What do you think of evil in the world?
25. What are your ideas of an afterlife?
26. If God could grant you any three wishes, what would they be?

(Daniel A. McKeever, "The Religious History: A Pastoral Instrument." Unpublished master's thesis, Southern Baptist Theological Seminary, 1971.)

I would add to these two additional questions:

1. What kinds of experiences in prayer or hindrances to prayer are you having now?
2. What is your greatest temptation?

The crucial issue in the pastoral use of groups is: Does this group come to grips with the person's relationship to God in relation to his neighbor? This can be explicit or implicit, verbal or nonverbal, but not *all* of either. The therapeutic strategies mentioned earlier in this chapter are not "pasted together" in some willy-nilly eclecticism. Rather they are critically assessed in the light of their theological meaning as both the individual and the group exist separately and together before God. The pastor is concerned with the person's need for intimacy in the group and his need for solitude and privacy before God apart from anyone. The pastor holds this polarity in tension and inviolate because of the very nature of prayer: it is both corporate and individual. It goes awry when it is only the one and never the other.

Prayer Groups

The group-counseling movement among pastors has tended to leave the prayer group to the arch-fundamentalists and to those who experiment with faith healing, spiritualism, and/or extrasensory perception. The straightforward group whose members confer with one another about their most negative prayers of anger, desolation, and feelings of abandonment in relation to God is a vital possibility for a pastoral group. If the group includes humor in the orbit of prayer and can share laughter in relation to God, then its vitality is increased. (John Bill Ratliff, "Humor as a Religious Experience." Unpublished doctoral dissertation, Southern Baptist Theological Seminary, 1970.) Prayer itself can be seen as a childish dependency of a child state, or as a parental state in which one points out things to God and paternalizes the less fortunate, or it can be seen as an adult walk with God.

In all these forms of group counseling, the pastor uniquely focuses whatever the theories of group formation have to offer upon the main *raison d'être* of a pastor and his church: the increase of the love of God and neighbor, both in community and in solitude. In doing so, he can equilibrate the tension within himself between group and individual counseling.

Chapter 10

THE NUCLEAR FAMILY AND
THE LARGER FAMILY OF MANKIND

A final dilemma is always with the pastor as a counselor. The dilemma is that of the tension between his responsibility to care for the nuclear family, on the one hand, and his prophetic and pastoral responsibility to free people from bondage to family idolatry and to give them a vision of and relationship to the larger family of mankind. By definition the nuclear family means the tight-knit relationship of father, mother, son, daughter, brother, sister, and grandparents. This might be called a "blood-kin" definition of the family. By the larger family of mankind we mean people of all races, creeds, and conditions of life both geographically and socially. The larger family of mankind includes both "Jew and Gentile, bond and free, male and female," in the larger macrocosm of humankind. One could see this as kinship by creation of all human creatures, or one could see it as Harry Stack Sullivan described it when he said that we are all more distinctly human than otherwise.

The built-in tension between the nuclear family and the larger family of mankind deeply involves the nature of religion at its best. Freud stated the three positive functions of religion in the family this way: (1) Religion, apart from pathological phenomena, lowers the importance of the family of parents and siblings. (2) Religion provides a sublimation and safe ethical mooring for one's sexual impulses. (3) Religion gives a person access to the larger family of mankind. In between the tight-knit nuclear family and the larger family of mankind is the "extended family" of the church, school, and/or neighborhood. (Sigmund Freud, "The History of an Infantile Neurosis," in *Standard Edition of the Complete Psychological Works of Sigmund Freud*, tr. and ed. by James Strachey with others, Vol. 17, pp. 114–115; London: The Hogarth Press and Institute of Psychoanalysis, 1959.)

The pastor is a counselor in the context of the church. The brunt of the stress between the nuclear family and the larger family of mankind—people of other neighborhoods, schools, and churches, people of other races, "strangers," outcasts from the nuclear family and the extended family—falls upon the church and its ministry. The pastoral counselor bears the ambiguity of encouraging the development of close affectionate ties within the nuclear family and at the same time sustaining people as they break away from the family to establish their own autonomy, as they see members of their own family reject, ostracize, or desert one another, and as the inevitable forces of illness, aging, and death break up the nuclear family. More than this, the pastoral counselor is the representative of the "larger family of mankind." He takes his stand against the idolatry of the parent-sibling family to the exclusion of people of other faiths, other races, different moral standards, different social classes and conditions that make them bachelors—male or female—widows and widowers, divorcées, etc. Many people are alone and without a nuclear family in the present. They are often without an extended family.

To omit or overlook this source of stress in the day-to-day work of the pastoral counselor means failure to account for the large percentage of the counseling that a pastoral counselor does. The problems associated with the pull and tug among the nuclear family, the extended family, and the larger family of mankind compose from 60 to 70 percent of the cases encountered by pastoral counseling. This fact has been established in several surveys of the presenting difficulties of persons seeking pastoral counseling.

Biblical Perspectives of the Family

The Old Testament and the New Testament present contrasts of attitudes toward the family. The family is the beating heart of the Jewish faith. In the Old Testament there are nearly three hundred references to the family or the tribe, whereas the word "family" is rarely used in the New Testament. Both the parent-sibling family and the extended family of the Jewish people often became self-contained units in a hostile world. Stories such as those of Naomi and Ruth, of the flight of Jonah, of the healing of Naaman the Syrian, reflect a prophetic outreach toward the larger family of mankind who were not familially or ethnically related.

However, the main thrust of Hebrew thinking in the Old Testament was determined by the Hebrews' strong sense of destiny as God's chosen people. From among them would come, one day, the Messiah. He would be raised up as the seed of Abraham. "Every Hebrew carried that seed in his loins. It was his duty to propagate it, to beget sons and pass on the sacred torch from generation to generation. Begetting children was, therefore, a man's primary response to God. No wonder, therefore, that family life was the central focus of the Hebrew society. No wonder all Hebrew men were expected to marry and to raise a family." (David R. Mace, *The Christian Response to the Sexual Revolution*, p. 19; Abingdon Press, 1970.) In the absence of a clearly defined concept of personal immortality, the perpetuity of a man depended quite heavily upon the birth of children, especially sons. They bore his name. In the Hebrew conception of sexual reproduction, the womb of a woman was simply a receptacle, a vessel, an incubator, to receive the seed from a man. There was no idea of the sperm and ovum uniting to form a zygote for the beginning of human life. The man contributed the seed. The woman received it. In a mysterious way, however, direct intervention from God was necessary for "opening the womb," so that the seed of man could enter. As David Mace again says: "A man's seed became his child, wherever planted. Since the woman contributed nothing of her essential self for the child she bore, but merely provided an incubator for its early growth, her role in the drama of reproduction was essentially a subsidiary one. This, rather than an inferior strength or intelligence, is probably the fundamental reason why women were considered in the ancient world to be less important than men." (*Ibid.*, p. 26.) Consequently, a man and a woman who were husband and wife were caught up together in a destiny. They and their children were bound together in the profoundly centralized unit of the family. The family and progeny became the primary value of the Hebrew man or woman. Contrary to contemporary attitudes toward the military, the family took precedence over military service. The Hebrew bridegroom was exempted from serving in the military until he had had time to get down to the business of getting his wife pregnant and seeing to it that he had children to assure that his name and line would be continued. He was given this chance before he was expected to fight in battles defending his country. The continuity of the blood-kin line and the continuity of the Hebrew race as a people took precedence over everything else.

In the life and teaching of Jesus, however, one finds considerable contrast and challenge to the basic Hebrew attitude toward family which has just been described. In Jesus' own relationship to the family, of which he was a part during his earthly pilgrimage, enough glimpses are provided the reader of the Gospels to get a consistent picture. The traditional near-idolatry of family and progeny was challenged by Jesus, and the creation story was reinterpreted.

Love, protection, and wise guidance of little children were primary in the teachings of the Gospels and of the apostle Paul. The messenger of the Lord told Zechariah that his son, John the Baptist, by his wife, Elizabeth, would "turn the hearts of the fathers to the children" (Luke 1:17). Jesus called little children unto him and blessed them. He watched as they played funeral and feigned grief, and as they piped and danced in the marketplace. He likened entry into the Kingdom of Heaven to the birth process and to becoming as a little child. He himself became a little child. He was reverential, though not cringing, toward his parents. When he was twelve years old he demonstrated considerable independence of them. Yet he was "obedient to them." At the wedding in Cana of Galilee, Jesus and his mother were present. He was somewhat stern with her, it seems to me, when he said: "O woman, what have you to do with me? My hour has not yet come." (John 2:4.) As he began his ministry, Jesus announced his mission at his home synagogue in Nazareth. He immediately ran into conflict with this extended family of which he and his parents and siblings were a part. As he continued his early ministry, his mother and his brothers came and sent for him. When told that they were outside asking for him, he said, "Who are my mother and my brothers?" Looking around on those who sat with him, he said: "Here are my mother and my brothers! Whoever does the will of God is my brother, and sister, and mother." (Mark 3:31–35.) It seems to me that Jesus was putting the primacy of the larger family of the Kingdom of God above the earthly family. He was lowering the importance of the earthly family and had gained access to the larger family of mankind under the sovereignty of God.

One cannot develop a one-sided interpretation of Jesus' teachings. He took seriously the ambiguity of the relationship of the tight-knit nuclear family and the larger family of mankind. Yet he also upbraided the Pharisees for having taken that which would have sustained and helped their parents and for having given it to the bureaucracy of Judaism. He chided them for no longer permitting persons to do anything for their father and mother. Thus they made void the word of God through their tradition which they sought to hand on. (Mark 7:9–13.) Jesus from the cross saw both his mother and the disciple whom he loved standing near and asked her to behold her son and told the disciple to behold his mother. The disciple took Jesus' mother to his own home. These accounts show remarkable balance between affectionate ties of one's relationships to one's nuclear family and one's commitment to encompass in his affections also the larger family of mankind. They are characterized by a stern tenderness.

In summary, the Christian revolution sustained the values of the intimate funds of affection that nourish human life at its earliest beginnings in the nuclear family. At the same time, Christians challenged the idolatry of the family as the be-all and end-all of existence. Jesus said that in the resurrection there will be neither marriage nor giving in marriage. (Luke 20:35.) Therefore, the pastoral counselor must discipline his tendency to absolutize the relative nature of the nuclear family. He works in the interfaces between the ambiguity that exists between the nuclear family, the extended family, and the larger family of mankind.

The Challenges of Premarital Pastoral Counseling

In the face of the sexual revolution of today, the overwhelming majority of people who decide to get married turn to a minister for the rituals of performing the ceremony. Therefore the opportunity for premarital counseling is prevalent in all these instances, although it may be very difficult to actualize.

Several massive social changes have occurred since about 1960 that have altered the whole context in which a pastor does premarital counseling.

First, the counterrevolution—which has been crudely nicknamed "the hippie movement"—in spite of some of its ephemeral characteristics, has left one more or less enduring impact on the interpretation of the family. The communal type of family relationship has accented one side of the ambiguity about which we are speaking in this chapter, namely, the movement beyond the nuclear and the expanded family to group relationships of men and women with each other in a larger commune.

Second, technology has advanced birth control through the use of "the pill" and more recently through the perfection of antiseptic and safe procedures for abortion. These technologi-

cal advances, combined with the legalization of abortion, reduce the fear of pregnancy and resulting feminine dependency
more than they have reduced the possibility of pregnancy. In
reality, nevertheless, they have introduced a realism into permissive premarital sexual behavior that did not previously
exist.

Third, living together prior to marriage has itself become a
form of self-help in premarital preparation. Increasing numbers of persons, many of whom perceive themselves to be
genuinely devout religiously, look upon premarital sexual behavior as a way to get to know each other rather than as a
prize or reward for having restrained their sexual needs prior
to marriage for chastity's sake. If a pastor today has a halo
of self-righteousness about chastity, in both men and women,
he certainly needs a good welding job to hold the halo in place
if he does much serious premarital counseling today. Living
together is a fact of action going on in the lives of many people
who come to a minister for a wedding ceremony.

Fourth, divorce and short-term commitments to marriage itself have become twin forces in the "belief systems" of persons
of all ages today. The first has become the *modus operandi*
for the second. Divorce is a much more casual experience for
many people than it is for ministers. Many ministers will hold
private belief systems concerning divorce, but for public role
performance purposes they will stay with a much more stereo-
typed set of beliefs. The personal and the institutional stress
shows itself in the pastor's life here too. Nevertheless, this
affects the premarital pastoral counseling of a pastor in that he
is increasingly being asked to perform the weddings of persons
who have been married one or more times previously. He has
his options of taking a forensic-legal attitude, a teaching-
reconciliation attitude, a growth–human potential attitude, or
a quick laissez-faire attitude. When confronted with the variety
of premarital pastoral counseling situations, he may find himself shifting from one to another of these attitudes. But shifting
is a way of coping with tension arising out of the ambiguity of
his commitment to the nuclear family, on the one hand, the

extended family of the church, on the other hand, and both of these in relationship to the larger family of humanity.

Fifth, women's liberation and women's power movements have changed the substance of premarital counseling. These movements include responses to the changed competence of women in the economic support of themselves, the changed awareness of their identity as persons in their own right existing not by reason of relationship to a man, their own selfhood, and the increased control they have over their own bodies because of more effective contraceptives and the legalization of abortions. These responses have effectively challenged the neat packaging of roles for men and women which were previously the topic of premarital counseling. Equal opportunity work laws and the increased earning ability of women have created a movement toward feminine independence that probably is here to stay. The pastor in premarital counseling, even with relatively nonsophisticated persons, is both presented with and should present the couple with the issues raised by the increased awareness of women of themselves as persons in their own right.

Some Varieties of Premarital Counseling

One of the major pitfalls for pastors is the unrealistic assumption that all premarital counseling has to follow one set pattern. Since Biblical times there have been varieties or alternative life-styles with reference to marriage. No monolithic pattern for premarital counseling, therefore, is clinically viable. Furthermore, under the varied "terrain conditions" of his day-to-day work, the wise pastor knows that there are many viable but different expectations for premarital pastoral counseling and care. I would identify these alternative life-styles and varieties of expectations as follows:

Old Friends and Relatives

Many of the people who come to a pastor and ask him to exercise his legal right to perform a wedding ceremony are old friends and/or relatives of his. He tends to have a much less formal relationship to these persons and a longer and more varied knowledge of them. However, the walls of personal privacy between him and them are thicker because he does not have the degree of objectivity, detachment, and anonymity that would enable a couple to reveal themselves to him most adequately. Therefore a good procedure to follow is to have the more formal kind of counseling done by a person who is not so closely related to them. The minister who performs the wedding ceremony then joins in the festivities of the occasion as a member of the family or as a friend of the family. At the very best, this kind of premarital pastoral relationship is difficult to manage, laden with anxiety, and somewhat confused. Clashing of informal and formal relationships and expectations is one of the causes of this.

"The Wedding Is the Thing"

In the highly structured, ritualized life-style of socially prominent families, "the wedding is the thing." Daughters and mothers, prospective mothers-in-law, and the circle of women friends of the bride plan for weeks and even months in an increasing crescendo of preoccupation with the wedding itself, the parties, luncheons, showers, and shopping that go with it. The groom tends to "go along" in a sort of grunting compliance. Heavy preoccupation with the social activities effectively insulates the cognitive and the emotional life of the bride and groom from any genuinely serious preparation for the more mundane, less dramatic, and deeply personal responsibilities that marriage itself will indubitably produce. Frankly, the pastor simply has to do the best he can to wedge his way into the attention of the couple with the critical issues confronting them in marriage. Counseling is better done with a couple after the fact of the wedding itself, in an early marriage-adjustment-growth group. The realities of marriage seem to hit these people harder. Life is not one long wedding party. The tragic element of this kind of situation, however, is the tendency of the feminine community to make the wedding a be-all and end-all in itself that glosses over a need for an intimate marriage, sacrifices contemplative moments of good judgment for social exhibition purposes, and exhausts both the bride and the groom to such an extent that fatigue short-circuits their relationship as husband and wife.

The "Here and Now" Wedding

A considerable number of persons who reach out to a minister for the performance of their ceremony want simply that —a wedding ceremony. They have little conception of their need of pastoral guidance and premarital counseling. They tend to show up at the last minute. They want the pastor to perform the ceremony at that very moment. Many times these persons are total strangers to the pastor, the church, and even the larger community. They come from other places. Several kinds of social dynamics cause this kind of demand upon the pastor.

First, there are those persons who come from the lower classes of society, both rural and urban, who are not educated or affluent enough either to know about or to be able to afford the protocol, the etiquette, and the rituals of more sophisticated weddings. The engagement is not their method of announcing an intention of marriage. Rather, the technique of elopement is the method used. Elopement is practical, less expensive, and free of publicity. Many times these persons are quite reliable and "salt of the earth" kinds of folk. Sometimes they may be literally running from disapproving parents, or hurrying into a panic wedding because of pregnancy or the military draft. Or they may even be intoxicated with alcohol or on a "drug trip." The pastor can, in a relaxed interview, diagnose these.

Second, these persons may be divorced persons who are remarrying. They do not want the publicity that would go with a wedding in their own community. Occasionally one sees this in widows and widowers who likewise do not want a public wedding.

Third, a minister may discover that some very prominent

persons in the political and entertainment world will use this kind of approach to their wedding in order to avoid publicity.

In all instances, the common denominator seems to be that the persons are seeking privacy, they are in a hurry, and they are usually strangers to him. Many of them have quite legitimate needs for privacy; all of them should be slowed down for a leisurely opportunity to become acquainted with the pastor as a person. In some instances, couples are likely to be in such a hurry that they do not want to be related to the pastor except as a public servant who happens to be on duty at their beck and call.

The pastor who confronts this kind of "here and now" wedding demand is fortunate if the couple will take time to talk with him in a one-interview guidance situation. My practice has always been that if they are in too big a hurry to do this, I refuse to marry them. Other men's practice varies. Ordinarily when couples are made to feel at home, put at ease, and treated with kindness, they tend to appreciate the minister's spending an hour or even more with them conversing about their life situation. The objectives of such an interview would be to discover who they are, where they come from, how they can be related to people in their own community for pastoral, medical, and other types of care that a newly married couple will need. They can occasionally provide the names of persons to whom the minister can write and advise that they are returning to the community and would appreciate their care. A pastor, a lay leader in a church, a physician, a business person —responsible people who could continue to be related to them as they seek to implement their plans for marriage and family.

The "After the Fact" Wedding

Some of the persons seeking a wedding ceremony have already been maritally related to each other without benefit of either a religious or a civil ceremony. In some states, common law recognizes these as authentic marriages between consenting adults. In others, the relationship of man and

sible people. Abortion has been taken for granted by the rich
for many years. In the minds of professional people abortion
has been a counsel of desperation to give desperate persons of
the middle and lower classes a second chance. Abortion is now
becoming a casual convenience for the careless and irresponsible, since it is financially feasible for the middle classes. Abortion has been the last recourse of the poor and the deprived
as a defense against starvation and death of mothers who had
no way to care for their babies. The easy generalizations of
propagandists on all sides of the abortion issue are usually
half-truths. The dilemma of abortion, more than any other,
shows the cleavage between the nuclear family and the extended family of the church and community. I find myself in
agreement with Mace that Christians are under obligation to
find a better way than abortion while we exercise patience
with the hard reality that it is here and is out in the open. The
social issues involved in the problem of abortion cannot be
neatly sidestepped in the name of a supposed counseling neutrality. Still another alternative is that of carrying the child to
full term and adopting it out to another family. The pastor does
not use marriage or any of these other alternatives as "advice,"
because these are permanent life decisions in any case. However, he can explore with the couple what *they* have thought
about these alternatives. He can use delaying procedures to
enable the couple to make a reflective, well-thought-out decision rather than an impulsive one. He might even ask them to
think it over, to sleep on it, to talk it over privately. One day's
time will not make any real difference.

The Leisurely Spiritual Pilgrimage

The most nearly ideal premarital pastoral counseling happens when a couple tell a pastor as much as six months to a
year ahead of time about their plans to be married. He may be
one of the very first persons to whom they tell their good news.
They ask him to do several things: to schedule counseling sessions with them as a couple; to collaborate with them in making their wedding plans; to perform their wedding ceremony.

woman has no legal status at all; neither do children b
the union. Such marriages have always been true of t
tremely poor and the extremely wealthy. In more
counter-culture thinking, for middle-class couples, livi
gether *is* their own do-it-yourself experiment to prepare
for marriage. Then, because of their own needs, their
to have children, their desire to relieve the strain on
friends and relatives, etc., they may decide to get m
officially. The wedding ceremony is "after the fact" c
marital union of the couple.

I am confident that much good can be done in one-inte
situations. It is a specialized kind of crisis intervention o
tunity. Strategically the pastor can attempt to diagnos
situation, and can seek to provide additional alternativ
the case of impulse.

Another "after the fact wedding" is the case in which
bride is already pregnant. The first thing a pastor shoul
is whether or not the woman has been told by a physician
she is pregnant. Premarital pregnancies are occasionally
diagnosis," for example. A visit with a nearby physician c
be helpful before they let their self-diagnosis push them
marriage on an impulse.

In the event that the pregnancy is a medically establi
fact, the pastor can converse with the couple about whe
they *really* care for each other and want to do so on a
manent basis in marriage. He can explore the other alte
tives they have considered or may not have thought of
The girl's remaining single and keeping the child is becor
more prevalent. Abortion is used by many. Abortion has b
technologically perfected and is being legally sanctio
David Mace estimates that in 1974 there will probably
1,600,000 known legal abortions in this country. He says
as Christians this is something we are going to have to
with whether we like it or not, but as Christians we
responsible for asking and seeking a better way. The wor
lawyer who pleads the case for abortion says that it sho
be a last-resort procedure and not the first option of irresp

Here a leisurely spiritual pilgrimage develops. They face each great issue of their marriage. I use the vows of the traditional wedding ceremony as a format for the several sessions (which always vary in number) that we have together. The format looks somewhat like this:

1. "To Have and to Hold"—The Communication of Tenderness and Considerateness
2. "From This Day Forward"—Freedom from the Tyranny of the Past
3. "For Better for Worse"—Celebrating and Comforting
4. "For Richer for Poorer"—Getting and Spending
5. "To Love and to Cherish"—Joint Decision-Making, Give-and-Take, and Learning to Treasure Each Other
6. "Till Death Us Do Part"—The Permanence of Covenant

The pastor also can use the plans for the wedding itself to explore the relationships of the couple to their parents, to enable the couple to evaluate their feelings about close friends who will be in the wedding, to get an overview of their "larger family" in terms of whom they invite to the wedding, and to coach them in how they use their money for the wedding, the reception, the formal meals, and the honeymoon.

A whole separate volume can be written on the subject of premarital counseling. Most of what is written is out of date now. One common failing of much that is written is that it is adaptable to persons in the upper classes and overlooks the varieties of life-styles of persons who are neither highly educated nor affluent. The point of view here is to underscore some of the varieties and to encourage greater maneuverability in the attitude and technique of pastors in premarital guidance and counseling.

PASTORAL COUNSELING IN THE PROCESS OF MARRIAGE CONFLICT

Once a couple are past the wedding, tensions begin to appear between the privacy they have with each other as a couple and the demands of their parents-in-law, their social groups of peers, their interactions with the larger extended family of church and school and with the even larger community. The pastor, representing both their personal and private needs for a secure family and their larger public needs to be a part of a wide, wide world, becomes a minister of reconciliation, an interpreter, and a negotiator alongside the couple in the community.

The pastor's work as a marriage counselor is done within the shaping environment of the group life of the church. Therefore family life education groups are a necessary part of the work of the pastor as a marriage counselor. He cannot, however, with safety to the families involved, conduct such groups unless he is also ready and able to provide individual counseling to persons who have problems that cannot be dealt with in the group context. Genuine safeguards also must be set up to protect the interests and needs of persons in the church who are single, widowed, or divorced. Pronounced emphases upon the "family-centered church" tacitly exclude these persons. The church idolatrously centers on the importance of the nuclear family when this happens. The sovereignty of Christ and his concern for the larger family of mankind challenges the subtle presuppositions upon which much family-centered thinking rests. (More detailed discussion of these problems will be found in the following resources: Clark E. Vincent, *Readings in Marriage Counseling*, Thomas Y. Crowell Company, 1957; David R. Mace, *The Christian Response to the Sexual Revolution*, Abingdon Press, 1970; Nathan W. Ackerman, *The Psychodynamics of Family Life: Diagnosis and Treatment of Family Relationships*, Basic Books, Inc., 1958.)

The point of concentration here is the process of conflict within marriage that leads ultimately to divorce and the specific steps a pastor can take to anticipate, stop, reverse, or set aright the process of marriage conflict. The pastor discovers that the persons who come to him for pastoral care and counseling on marriage difficulties usually do so only after their difficulties are in advanced stages of deterioration.

This suggests two basic principles of pastoral counseling which call for careful research. First, marriage conflict goes through a process that can be observed, charted, identified, and described. Second, the process itself happens within the interacting field of many persons in the family, church, and community. The couple themselves are only two among many people. The pastor is one among many people who are giving advice, counseling, and exerting influence. The process of conflict tends, therefore, to be conditioned by the kind and quality of communication between and among these persons.

With these two principles in mind, I spent two days a week for eighteen months working with seventy-three couples in a counseling service that I initiated. My purpose was to see what needed to be done pastorally for persons at the different stages of marital conflict and disintegration. I identified what these stages were, what characterized them, and with what understanding a pastor should be endowed as he counsels people at the varying stages of stress.

The Process of Marriage Conflict

Marriage conflict moves from the typical "growing pains" of marital adjustment through serious assaults upon the covenantal nature of the marriage to chronic conflict as a way of life and/or to acute conflict as a problem-solving experience. This latter problem-solving experience can result either in divorce or in personality change, based on mutual insight and understanding in the instance of creative conflict. Nowhere does the tension between the close-knit, nuclear family, the expectations and rules of the extended family of the churches, and the great forces of society as a whole surface more clearly than in the process of marriage conflict. Marital conflict can be charted as moving through at least seven definable stages:

1. The Stage of Typical Adjustmental Conflicts

Early marriage is filled with the conflicts that "are common to all marriages." If a couple do *not* have conflict over these things, one might guess that they are leaving some of their "homework" undone. One might ask if the conflicts are actually going on and they are not aware of them. This happens very easily when the couple are enjoying the first glow of sexual freedom in marriage. But these conflicts are both tangible and intangible.

The more tangible conflicts arise over such problems as when to have the first experience of intercourse, who will accept full responsibility for birth control—the husband or the wife—and how much money will be spent on the honeymoon. The husband, for instance, can be extremely anxious about spending money staying in a hotel that has "atmosphere" and decor when a good commercial hotel is cheaper. In other words, he will be penny-wise and feeling-foolish. The nonrecurring aspect of his expenses here will not occur to him. Usually people are married only once. They are married the *first* time only once in every instance!

When the couple return home, the tangible problems take a new form. Whether or not the wife works, what will happen if she becomes pregnant, where they are going to live, and the adequacy or inadequacy of the arrangements for living quarters made prior to marriage—these are just a few of them. Whereas the fears and anxieties of courtship and engagement were relatively abstract, they become more concrete and tangible in marriage. Fatigue and preoccupation can, as a result, become the atmosphere of the first few weeks of marriage.

But the obvious tangibility of these problems should not obscure six necessary adjustments which are not so apparent. These persist from the beginning to the end of any marriage and are the hinges upon which the whole thing swings:

a. *The development of an agreed-upon schedule of work, rest, play, lovemaking, and worship.* A steady course has to be driven between being overscheduled and simply leaving the whole matter of time and schedule-planning to chance. The earliest quarrels in a marriage tend to center on failures to synchronize masculine and feminine uses of time. For example, the husband may sleep late in the morning and go to bed late; the wife may get up early and go to bed early. A couple like this can, conceivably, go a whole week and never talk with each other, much less have sex relations.

b. *The development of a deeper-level and mutually satisfying plan of communication.* The couple should "pause for station identification" daily, weekly, monthly, and yearly to sketch out the schedules of these blocks of time, gear them in with their overall goals and aspirations, and simply get to know each other as persons. They actually learn to talk with each other in a dramatically verbal way. Up to now they have depended upon kisses, motions of the body and hand, and the rituals of making dates and going places. But now the question is, Can they stay in the same room with each other for an evening of conversation? Do they lay plans for their lives together or do they just throw their minds out of gear and let their lives go where circumstances push them?

c. *The development of a comradely understanding as to their masculine and feminine identities, i.e., what a man is "supposed to be" and what a woman is "supposed to be."* More than this, under God they should develop an understanding of why it is he made them in his image and yet created them as male and female. They thus find out what they are to *be,* and the everyday tasks of life are shaped according to this identity, their *being* man and woman. This calls for real conflict. The new confrontation in the intimacy of marriage calls for personal ability to learn from each other. The things they have "always thought" are necessarily reshaped by the greater truths about what *this* man and *this* woman conceive their function *as* man and *as* woman to be. This confrontation brings to the surface their parents' ideas about the roles of men and women. For example, the wife who works will have very different feelings about the management of money as compared with those of the mother of her husband, who never worked outside the home. Likewise, the husband, having been raised by that mother, will have different expectations of the wife from those her father had of her mother, especially if her mother worked full time and the father was an invalid. These things must be

talked over and worked through. Much conflict attends the
process. The major issues of the liberation of women today are
the stuff of which much conflict is made, particularly if these
are the academic covers for an inherently sibling-competition
relationship. Apart from such a power struggle, the issues of
the liberation of women can be a source of creative growth.

d. *The establishment of an adult-to-adult relationship to
parents-in-law.* A couple bring their separate family histories
to the marriage with them. Their reactions to their parents
become old molds for their reactions to each other as representatives of the opposite and of the same sex. Their reactions
to their siblings, if any, become patterns of conflict and cooperation, competition and collaboration for their relationship
to each other. Their major task is to learn to look at these old
reactions, to laugh at them, and to help each other discard
them. More than this, their task is to believe in themselves and
in each other enough to be assured that new patterns of reaction can be developed. Games *can* be called off, and intimacy
can take their place.

e. *The growth of fellowship with other married couples and
with unmarried persons.* This is especially crucial in the emphases upon "open" marriage, and in the involvement of men
and women—not married to each other—on the job. Women
and men not married to each other often spend much more
time together than they do with their spouses. When a spouse
—husband or wife—expects these work relationships to be de-
personalized and free of any human emotions, conflict with the
mate is about to happen. They are just not this way. Here the
place of work presents the "larger family" tension. These things
must be talked over and worked through. Much conflict attends
the process.

f. *The development of a spiritual welcome and joyous acceptance of the first child in the family.* The early, typical
adjustments of the couple are consummated in the incorpora-
tion of the first child into the life of the family. The word "in-
corporate" is used advisedly. It literally means to "embody
the child" into the life of the family as a whole. Either all

other conflicts of schedule, communication, and masculine and feminine identity are faced before the coming of the child or they become forced issues when the first child comes. The element of option in adjustment is now removed. A baby with a high temperature does not ask if the father is accustomed to going to bed early. A baby yet two months before birth does not ask whether the family can get along without the mother's paycheck. A baby who is hungry at two in the morning does not ask whether Daddy would prefer that Mother be out at a party or giving baby her full attention! In other words, the adjustment of parenthood removes fantasies of freedom from the minds of a couple. Parenthood demands that they accept responsibility of the freedom they have already exercised in creating a child. As has been said, the whole problem of *whether* to have children at all is an open question today in ways that it was not before.

Formerly, a pastor could assume that all couples who married took the possibility of having children as an inherent part of the decision to marry. This is no longer the case. With the population explosion, the pill, legalized abortion, and the increased independence of women, *whether or not* a couple will *ever* have children is an open question and often a source of deep conflict.

Basic changes should and must take place in the life of a married couple during the years prior to the birth of the first child. Left unattended or unmet, these conflicts will form the basis for the symptoms that emerge in the later states of conflict.

Technique and Procedures. Group counseling at this normative stage of conflicts is the optimum technique to use. A didactic springboard for discussion is usually all that is needed to get a group going, such as: "How do you plan the use of time, money, and energy so as to deepen your love for each other?" Couples need socialization with other couples who are facing the same problems in order to offset their isolation. Individual help can be given to couples who are struggling with intimate problems they do not want to share in the group. Right here the ambiguity between a nuclear family and a larger family of others is enacted in the individual and group counseling. (See Howard Hovde, *The Neo-Married;* Judson Press, 1968.)

When a couple do seek pastoral counseling during this stage of conflict, they tend to come to the interview *as a couple.* They refer to themselves as "we" and to their conflicts as "ours." The techniques of conjoint family counseling are highly useful. The objectives of counseling at later stages of conflict, when the couples are alienated and estranged from each other, point toward getting this kind of dialogue to happen. (See Virginia Satir, *Conjoint Family Therapy: A Guide to Theory and Technique,* rev. ed.; Science and Behavior Books, Inc., 1967.)

2. The Stage of a Disrupted Covenant

Attitudes and Behavior. Marriage is a covenant of trust. Legal complications occur only later after the covenant of trust has been disrupted. The second phase of marital conflict is the disruption of the covenant of trust. It may be even more serious than this: the covenant may have been defective from the beginning and only now does this become apparent. For example, a husband withholds the fact that he has a criminal record, that he must report to a parole officer, and that he cannot buy real estate because he has no rights as a citizen until he is off parole. He does not tell his wife this. She discovers it several months later when they attempt to buy a house. Or the wife does not tell the husband that she has been previously married and that she continues a clandestine relationship with her former husband upon his occasional return to town. These are *defective covenants,* i.e., they were not openly arrived at and they represent matters large enough to undermine confidence in the integrity of the partner.

But ordinarily the covenant was established in something that approaches good faith, if not good faith itself. Then, because of a neglect of the problems mentioned above, the *willingness* of the partners to make the marriage work is called into question. They lose touch with each other and withdraw as selves from each other. Isolation increases and the degree of suspicion mounts in proportion to the isolation. Soon assaults are made upon each other's integrity: "I suppose you worked last night; I don't really know what you did." "It is hard for me to get through to you without yelling; I sometimes think you are just plain stupid." "Well, I would have told you what I was doing, but I knew you wouldn't believe me."

The hallmark of this stage of conflict is repeated failure of communication. The situation progressively deteriorates until the couple simply live in silence. Each partner talks about only the most superficial things and tends to go his separate way. Each feels that the other does not understand and does not want to understand, does not care and does not want to care. The only vestige of a covenant that remains is a mutual feeling of hopelessness: What are we going to do? Contact of selves, not communication, takes place through tears, profanity, or brutality. Occasionally violent efforts at overcoming the chasm are made by hyperactive sexual behavior between the estranged persons of the marriage. But this is not a communion of tenderness and respect. It is a hostile encounter in itself with the violent hope that passion itself will overcome the barrier of isolation.

Techniques and Procedures. At this stage of conflict the pastor ordinarily has little opportunity for counseling. He can, however, "listen" to nonverbal communication: The two people show up at church separately; they make cutting remarks on social occasions; they overabsorb themselves in work; they develop heavy involvements in work, in hobbies, and in play with members of each other's peer sex; they travel a lot but never go together; they may begin to drink excessively, etc. Careful note of these can be made.

A response that amounts to precounseling is the careful use of "bump-into" contacts, casual conversation at social gatherings, and close attention to crises such as illness, bereavement, the advent of a child, the appointment to a new job. These efforts tend to create an atmosphere of warmth and nonverbal awareness with the couple. No programmed technique or tool is very useful here. However, the pastor's own access to people at the very casual and informal levels of life—mixed liberally with personal sensitivity, effective observation powers, and much common sense—provides people with a kind of availability of help not found elsewhere.

The pastor is related also to other persons who know the couple and are concerned for a variety of motives with their marital interaction. Relatives, close friends, and neighbors who may not be close to them are "watchers" of their actions. Some of these people are often the first to talk with a pastor. This interacting field of relationships is the context of much pastoral counseling of married couples. The pastor walks a narrow ridge between allowing himself to be used by in-laws and friends, on the one hand, and reacting against them so much that the real assistance they can be is forfeited and/or unguided.

3. The Stage of Private Misunderstanding

Problems and Behavior. One thing characterizes the couple up to this point most significantly: the two have not verbally told anyone else of their distress. Up to this point they have kept up appearances. They have carefully covered for each other. They have even deceived for themselves and for each other. But the individual isolation, the loneliness, and the feeling of not being understood create a vacuum that must be filled.

Sometimes the distress is communicated through illness on the part of one or the other. Various organs of the body, depending upon the individual constitution, fall prey to disorders in one way or another. Stress may reactivate an old disease, such as a latent tuberculosis; it may introduce a new one in a previously healthy person; it may cause an already present one to mean more to the individual. Illness becomes the organizing center of each one's reactions.

At other times the marital distress is communicated and the vacuum of anxiety filled by behavioral reactions. Excessive spending is one form of allaying anxiety and at the same time expressing hostility. Alcohol or drugs become more useful in calming jittery nerves and giving depressed spirits a momentary lift. Contemporary advertising probes heavily into these weak spots in order to make sales and to create the illusion of security in desperately anxious persons. (Some attention to the ethical issues at stake in modern advertising needs to be given at this point as well as many others. Here is one vital point of connection between pastoral counseling and social ethics and the need for social change.)

Disease and behavior difficulties—such as alcoholism, drug addiction, excessive spending, absorption in cheap literature, and excessive soap-opera viewing—are accompanied by other symptoms of isolation. The husband may frequent prostitutes. The man or the woman may try to pick up strangers without revealing his or her identity. The man or the woman may temporarily revert to earlier homosexual pickup behavior. These behaviors are symptomatic of the private misunderstanding that has happened in the marriage itself. When, however, this loneliness and isolation become unbearable, one or both of the marital partners break away to someone in their environment with whom they feel they can talk.

Pastoral Techniques and Tools. When a couple begin to show nonverbal signs of desperation in their marriage, and the pastor is aware of their distress, he has the right to intervene with a letter, a telephone call, or a visit. If he has performed their wedding ceremony, he can act upon a covenant that pastors should regularly make with couples whom they marry, i.e., that if the couple begins to have trouble, the partners will seek his counsel and guidance, and if he becomes aware that they really are in distress, he will have the privilege given by the covenant to bring the subject up with them. Such prior "credit" in the relationship is the exception rather than the rule, however. Even without this, though, the pastor has a right to visit, to inquire, and to extend himself. He may be told that this is not the time for talking with others and that the partners want to "work at it themselves." Even in this case he has gone far in raising their motivation to do just that. He can be on standby, ready for them if and when they do need him, and he can assure them of a level of privileged communication at the same time.

Referral is another tool at this stage of conflict. The couple may look on the pastor as an insider rather than an outsider. They may say that he is too close to them, has been their friend for many years, and too much like a member of their family. He should be able to discern this intuitively himself. In this case, he can call on the resources of other counselors and sustain his most durable relationship. (See Wayne E. Oates and Kirk H. Neely, *Where to Go for Help,* Revised and Enlarged Edition; The Westminster Press, 1972.)

4. The Stage of Social Involvement

Problems and Behavior. As has been said, when the isolation and blackout on communication becomes too intense one or the other or both partners break out of the silence and talk with other people. This may be done wisely or unwisely, in a responsible or an irresponsible way. The tight-knit nuclear privacy is broken. The parental families and the larger circle of friends, work associates, and others flows in upon them. This swirling confusion of the family, the church, and the community as a whole is the arena of action of the pastor as a marriage counselor.

The couple may go to their parents for guidance, as they did in former years. Sometimes this is not possible. Instead, they may involve a brother or a sister who has been particularly close to them. The wisdom of doing this depends entirely upon the kind of persons these people are. Are they wise? Sometimes they are; often they are not. On the other hand, the couple may choose to go to a physician, a minister, or a former teacher. Marriage counseling is a cognate function of many different kinds of professions, and all these persons should be alert to the family overtones of the kinds of problems presented to them. The happiest thing that could occur at the time of the first breakout of the isolation is that the person would go to a responsible, wisely devout, and skilled person for understanding. A faithful pastor should pray for and be committed to a more and more sensitive and durable relationship of trust that will enable people to come to him at a time like this. For this is the most propitious moment when a married couple can best be helped; i.e., the pastor can be *the first person to whom the couple break away from the isolation of the stage of private misunderstanding.* Thus the processes of social involvement can be guided and kept at a reasonably constructive level.

But often this is not the way that the movement out of isolation occurs. Too often one or the other partner talks indiscriminately to anybody whom he or she meets. A random stranger on the telephone inquiring of the husband's whereabouts in order to buy a piece of merchandise from him is met with this: "I don't know where he is. He never tells me anything. Here I sit all day with these kids, too!" Or instead of this, the husband or wife, and sometimes both of them, finds another member of the opposite sex "who understands." The other person may or may not have unalloyed motives of his own. The partner may simply be looking for a little sexual pleasure or for someone whose mate he or she can further alienate. Ordinarily, though, this may begin in an honest attempt to be helpful and only gradually become more and more involved. The third party in every instance, however, becomes a part of the problem, and not the solution.

The thing we do with our more intimate personal friends when they present marital problems is to call for the help of a more detached person who can deal with them more professionally and less informally, for community gossip and extramarital involvements tend to be formed just this way. Often pastors say that we should beware of counseling with people about marriage difficulties, especially women, because we can become sexually involved too easily. One observes, however, that ministers do not get involved with counselees nearly as often as they do with their secretaries, educational directors, deacons' wives, and other persons who are associated with them in the distinctly administrative and personal aspects of their social lives. These persons come to the pastor in an uncontrolled informal relationship. The pastor thus becomes the "third person" in a marriage "triangle."

Techniques and Tools. The techniques and tools of pastoral counseling at this stage are too many, varied, and sophisticated to discuss in this brief section. Two major technical sources can be cited. *The Family Coordinator* is a journal devoted to the cross-disciplinary task of marriage counseling. Clifford Sager and Helen Kaplan have edited a serious work entitled *Progress in Group and Family Therapy* (Brunner/Mazel, Inc., 1972). However, several standard operating procedures are necessary for the parish minister, especially, to use.

First, the spouses tend to seek help individually at this stage of conflict. One or the other partner does not reach out for help. Yet the pastor is responsible to both partners. It is standard operating procedure to involve the other spouse either by sending word by the one who did come, by direct contact through a bump-into contact, a letter, a telephone call, or a formal visit, whichever tool has the least possibility of being distorted or misused. This must be done, with the permission of the partner who did come, before anything other than an initial one or two interviews can be promised wisely.

Second, if communication is extremely poor between the husband and wife, it is better that they be seen separately in individual counseling or together in group counseling rather than together as a couple. This should continue, in my opinion, until the communication has improved enough that they can talk together without saying things in an interview to hurt each other, things they would never dare say outside the interview with a third person present.

Third, the objective of the counseling, it seems to me, at this stage is fourfold: (1) to provide an opportunity for the joint identification of the couple with a person whose wisdom they both respect and whose affection they both can accept in trust; (2) to develop an overall view of the history and the ways of relating to each other that cause them to frustrate rather than satisfy each other's needs; (3) to provide a *reflective* rather than an *impulsive* approach to decision-making as a couple; and (4) to reduce the necessity for them to talk indiscriminately in the community by restricting this kind of conversation to the counseling sessions.

5. The Stage of Threats of Attempts at Separation

Problems and Attitudes. The marital conflict is further inflamed when separation is threatened or is seen as the only way out. Separation may take place on a socially acceptable plane, on a planned and legal basis, or on a chaotic and compulsive basis. Socially acceptable separations occur under the guise of changes of the husband's work. For example, the wife goes away for a long summer vacation, or the husband stays in town while she lives in the suburbs, or he may reactivate a military tour of duty. Many other stratagems may be available at the moment and may become socially acceptable foils for marital conflict.

Under professional guidance, or by reason of wisdom on each other's part, the couple may be led to plan a manifest, open, candid separation. They may do this while each of them is getting some counseling assistance. This is often done in order to prevent further infections from arising. It especially protects the children from scenes between the parents. But the objective of such separation is creative and usually aims at improving rather than dissolving the relationship. Sometimes the separation is set up on a legal basis for a cooling-off period to see if a divorce is really what is wanted. Many dramatic changes have been observed in formal, legal separations set up as a trial period for a divorce. In fact, some state laws recognize two years' separation as the most valid ground for divorce. From a legal point of view, and from a therapeutic point of view, this is one of the wisest conditions for divorce.

But the more common kind of separation is the chaotic one, done in anger, vindictiveness, or as a means of manipulation and coercion. One person walks out and goes home to his or her parents. Another kicks the partner out the first time the spouse comes home with alcohol on his or her breath. Another becomes violently outraged by an adventure in infidelity on the part of his wife. These become lighted torches that set the whole marriage on fire. In many of these instances, processes of vindictiveness that are irreversible are set in motion. Many times the separation is neither done nor taken seriously, but becomes a repeated form of transient petulance between immature people. But often the separation is only a prelude to the next phase of conflict.

Techniques and Tools. The essential tool in counseling at this stage is the refusal of the counselor to be a messenger between the partners. They are to do their own communication. The pastor refuses to be manipulated by either of them. He encourages them to take any positive move toward conciliation that seems constructive, and to avoid destructive "game" moves.

Another important tool is the weight of loneliness and its effect on changing self-perceptions. Also, extramarital involvements as a means of alleviating this loneliness come into focus for more objective appraisal.

Legal consultation, as in the case of the legal separation, can be an effective tool of counseling. Collaboration with a lawyer is often a means of informing the pastoral counselor as to legal "games" that the couple might be playing.

In the case of alcohol or drug abuse in husband or wife, the trial separation has been observed to be one way of "raising the bottom" for an alcoholic or a drug user to hit, as Alcoholics Anonymous puts it.

6. The Legal Phase of Marriage Conflict

Several signals indicate that this legal phase has set in, regardless of whether separation has taken place. They are sometimes subtle and sometimes obvious signals. The subtle signal appears in the kind of demand that is laid on a pastor, for example. He is expected to "decide who is to blame." The couple present their evidence and expect him, without the help of a judge, jury, or fee to function as a lawyer—to be a judge and a divider over them. The pastor does well to refuse this role as did Jesus in another connection when he said: "Who made me a judge or divider over you?" (See Luke 12:13 ff.) The pastor not only should be alert to this but should resist being pushed into this legal role. Such problems of affixing blame, for example, cut the pastor off from the person blamed. Lawyers do not mind this, but the pastor must be related durably to both partners, not legally and punitively to one at the expense of the other. More and more, however, lawyers are looking upon themselves as counselors-at-law and charging for services of counsel apart from specific "piecework" on legal papers drawn up. In these phases of conflict such problems emerge as feelings of hopelessness and self-depreciation on both sides. Economic anxiety and insecurity flood out much rational insight. The conflict of devotions between spouse and children rages. Social pressure from both sides forces "joiners" in sympathy for this spouse or that one. Few remain objective enough to be a part of the solution rather than the problem. The end result is that many divorced persons change their whole set of friends by moving to a new environment. (See William J. Goode, *After Divorce;* Free Press, 1956.)

One of the most helpful procedures to follow at this stage is to suggest that a legal separation be used as a trial period to test the couple's more positive feelings for each other and to test their willingness to face the realistic obstacles that divorce will later finalize. When couples get married, they really need an *engagement period* in which to test their decision to marry. When they start to dissolve their marriage, they need a *disengagement period* for similar testing of decisions before they are finally effected.

Another standard operating procedure is collaboration with the lawyer to get any advice and counsel as to how to keep from becoming a prejudicial combatant in the conflict. Also, the precise nature of child support, custody, and care is good information to have. (See Richard A. Gardner, *The Boys and Girls Book About Divorce;* Science House, Inc., 1970.)

Parents of couples this near to a marital dissolution themselves are in need of pastoral attention and grief-care. They often are severely wounded by the loss of their in-laws and stand helpless to care for their own grown daughter or son.

7. The Stage of Divorce

Competent studies of divorced persons indicate that the real shock and numbness of the grief situation occurs long before the actual granting of the divorce. We should not be deceived by the seeming lack of feeling that many demonstrate in the courtroom. Nor should we be enchanted by those few miracles that do occur when people are reconciled on the eve of the divorce decree and live happily ever after. Much that has happened has taken the marriage beyond the point of no return. Many things can yet be done, as we shall see, but not all of a sudden. People that belong together do not need to be glued together, but much has been done to separate them that is modifiable by wise pastoral care. This is not a hopeless situation, but it is a hard one.

Divorce is being viewed more and more casually. People tend *not* to be as upset by the experience as they were even ten years ago. However, this is deceptive. Some pastoral counselors in training will say: "She (or he) came in quite composed for the next interview after the divorce was granted. She (or he) acted as if nothing had happened." Five interviews and six weeks later, however, the same counselor often reports, e.g., "She was depressed today and wept profusely over her loss and hurt." Or, even two years later, a counselee may present an unrealistic scheme for remarrying the person he had divorced.

The thing the pastor must concentrate upon at the point of the decree of divorce is the next phase into which the couple goes almost immediately.

The Post-Divorce Bereavement Situation

More and more we are seeing pastoral care during critical incidents as a unique ministry to people in their losses. Divorce is a loss in much the same sense that death is. As has been said in connection with religious history, in a sense death is more easily assimilated than divorce. Death is clean, final, and definitive. Death cuts with a sharp knife. Divorce cuts with a dull, dirty, rusty knife. And it accentuates the poignancy of the grief. A flood of grief, characterized by much hostility and vindictiveness as well as by the tears of frustrated love and devotion, follows with a heavy depression of emotions. Loneliness and social awkwardness due to the new role and status as a divorced person complicate the process of readjustment. As one divorcé put it to me: "I feel more of a second-class citizen than any Negro in the South."

All this is compounded by the recharting of affections and the discovery of a new meaning in life apart from the previous marriage. Many find this meaning in their work, and this is easier for professional people than for nonprofessional ones. Others find the new meaning in their children, and this is much easier for mothers than for fathers. Some find new meaning in the life of their church, but this depends upon the conditions within the church itself. Others find new meaning in completely relocating and starting over where they are not known. Pioneer areas of the country are filled with divorced persons who have "amputated the past" to the best of their ability. Even so they are like men without a country or lost sheep of the house of Israel as far as their relationship to the churches is concerned. The majority of divorced people find new meaning in remarriage. This has become the prevailing pattern in our society. But it puts them in opposition to the church, whose teachings hitherto allowed these people no room.

The agenda of grief-therapy groups should include the loss of persons by divorce. Such persons are not just husbands and/or wives who have lost someone by divorce. The sons and daughters of divorced parents are often similarly cut off from those whom they love and whose love they want.

The foregoing discussion of the process of marriage conflict provides the groundwork for evolving some principles of pastoral counseling at the different stages of conflict. Obviously, the pastor must carefully reflect on the meaning of these different stages. Again, he must have a dynamic, developmental view of human life and the marriage relationship before this whole approach makes much rhyme or reason to him. He must learn to approach a marriage conflict situation not as a static, legal contract but as a personal covenant that is characterized by life, growth, deterioration, etc. This attitudinal orientation is best gained in a clinical setting where a staff of ministers discuss these problems. Reading this brief description of the stages can point one in this direction. However, the minister can compare his previous experience with what has been said here and learn much from his own experience. As he does this, he will see several principles emerging for devising specific techniques in a given situation.

The Principle of a Controlled Counseling Relationship

In everyday speech we talk of some situations as being "well in hand" and others of being "out of control." In a previous chapter we have examined the nature of controlled relationships. This needs repetition here because it is especially true of the pastor's relationship to a marriage conflict situation. As has been previously said, the initiative of the person *wanting* help in the marriage situation is required. This must be gained honestly and aboveboard, not covertly and surreptitiously. For example, if one partner of a marriage comes to the pastor, he or she may suggest that the pastor come by the home for a visit when the other partner is there "without that person's knowing that he knows about the trouble." This is a form of deceptiveness which should be avoided. It puts the pastor in the position of being manipulated by one partner against the other. Rather, the pastor would do much better to write, call, or visit on an aboveboard basis. Many counselors write a brief note to the other spouse. They do this with the permission of the person who did come to them. In such a note the counselor invites the other person to come by to see him. This leaves a large measure of freedom with the other spouse and at the same time clears the atmosphere of any covertness.

In addition to initiative, the pastor needs a place of discreet privacy, either in his home or in his study at the church, for conferences with the people who are having marriage difficulties. Furthermore, he needs enough time in which to do the work of counseling. For example, if the couple are demanding that he visit in the home and "settle things for them" at some late-evening hour, the pastor does well to interpret that conflict as a process of accumulated distress that will take time. Then after his visit in the home he can schedule further appointments in his office. Thus the pastor brings the whole situation under the control of his own professional relationship as to initiative, time, and place.

But these factors are external controls as compared with the distinctly spiritual awareness of the kind of relationship the pastor has to the individual or to the couple. The role of the pastor should be clearly and mutually understood. The person should understand perfectly that the pastor is not just another *neighbor* peering into the situation, not just another *friend* trying to be nice and friendly, not just another *relative* with a vested interest and a "side" in the matter, and not just a *preacher* looking for illustrations with which to dramatize his sermons. Rather, he is a *pastor* appointed by men and called by God to minister with confidence and commitment to all concerned. This role of his should be clear, lest his motives be interpreted wrongly. Otherwise, he could be seen as a competitor for the wife's affections. The wife, on the other hand, might see him as another man that the husband has "ganged up with" against a poor, defenseless woman. Both partners may see him as a father who is supposed to spank them and send them back to play peacefully. Or, as in the case of persons at the legal phase of the conflict, the pastor may be pushed into the role of judge and divider over them, to decide who is to blame and how the property should be divided. Clarity of role will facilitate communication, and the pastor must be explicit and forceful enough to make these things clear to the couple. When acute marital conflict is dealt with, passivity can be nondirectiveness, but more often it is irresponsibility.

Developing an Interprofessional Team

No matter how skilled a minister is, he cannot work effectively as a marriage counselor in isolation from other professional people. Such isolation goes hand in hand with failure. At the points of detection, diagnosis, treatment, and convalescence of his counselees, the pastor is deeply in need of colleagues such as the physician, the schoolteacher, the social worker, the lawyer, the judge, the juvenile probation officer, and the hospital official. For example, to expect each couple to have a thorough medical examination is often indicated. Specific medical problems have been discovered which either contributed to or caused the trouble. Early signs of mental illness can be checked by a physician as routine in such an examination. Specific medical therapies can be recommended to stabilize the situation while the counseling continues. Likewise, employers have been of vital assistance in work difficulties that aggravate the marital situation, and, in turn, pastoral assistance to the counselee has often made a better worker of the person. Public school teachers have often called stress situations to pastors' attention and, in turn, been coached by them on the needs of the children without the children ever being aware that their pastor was ministering indirectly to them through their teacher.

Identifying the Stage of Conflict

The pastor must carefully develop ways of identifying the stage at which he has found the conflict. *The kind of communication going on in the total situation is the basis of determining the stage.* For example, the couple in the typical adjustmental stage of conflict are likely to come to the pastor together. They will talk even with humor and a few tears about quarrels they have had, about their routine, their differing interpretations of the roles of men and women, their inability to talk with each other, and the like. But at the stage of serious conflict where the covenant has been threatened, they may never say anything to the pastor, although he may sense that something has gone wrong. He will see them come to different services at church for no obvious reason. They look unhappy. They may seek to depreciate each other, with humor, in a crowd or avoid the pastor, whereas they have hitherto been very open. He may hear about unusual things they have done that are not typical of their routine.

In the stage of private misunderstanding, the pastor may notice that the husband has bought a car that is just too expensive. The wife may have started dressing in a style that is out of keeping with her budget. The couple may go in over their head for a house. Or the counselor may detect the stress between the lines of a story about an illness. He may note that the couple have begun to drink or to drink more heavily.

When the couple do come to the pastor or open up to him when he goes to them, he can be assured that he has met them in the stage of social involvement. They probably talked with other people before they came to him. Therefore it is routine practice to ask: "Have you felt free to talk to anyone else?" From this point he can consult with them as to whether they *plan* to talk to anyone else. Thus he can bring some influence to bear upon regulating the communication processes. Localizing the spreading conflict is a major job. On the other hand, in certain situations the counselees really should confer with someone besides us, and this is ordinarily what we mean when we speak of referral. This does not mean sending the person away from us as if he was "beyond us." It means calling in the assistance of others. As representatives of the love of God in Christ, we are confident that neither the counselees nor the people whose assistance we seek for them are ever beyond his loving care.

Furthermore, when a couple have reached this stage they usually are not able to talk with each other meaningfully. Whereas in the earlier stages of conflict a pastor would see the couple together, he probably will want to schedule separate interviews with both husband and wife until the communication is clarified.

Stabilizing and Reversing the Process of Conflict

The next strategic objective of the pastor in dealing with marital conflict is to stabilize and reverse, if possible, the destructive process. For example, when an individual or a couple comes to the pastor in the stage of imminent divorce, they usually are coming out of desperation. He can free the situation a bit if he tells them that if they go ahead and get a divorce, he still wants to be a pastor to them. If they expect him to accept responsibility for conferring with them toward a reconciliation, they will necessarily have to "freeze" the divorce procedures until a considerably later date. He disavows any role as a miracle worker. He uses delaying procedures to create a free situation in which responsible counseling can take place.

In this situation, the pastor may, if he has succeeded in stabilizing the process just short of divorce, attempt to reverse it to the next-earlier stage. He may suggest that they confer with their lawyer as to the possibility of a *legal separation* as a basis for a divorce in the future if they so choose. This will give them time to try the new identity before they finally accept it. They can use the intervening time span for further counseling. This will assure them that they have done everything possible to work things out. It will give them a greater measure of freedom from later regrets. Sentimental appeals to the "good of the children," to the "poor mother's breaking heart," and to "how it will look for Christians to be divorced" simply galvanize the rebellious into action. The pastor can hasten the stampede by using such appeals. Appeals to their own self-esteem for having taken time to act wisely to seek counseling make much more sense.

When the couple come in at the stage of separation, the objective of the pastor is to keep it from further deterioration. But more than that, he looks back at the earlier stage and sees that his task is not to "glue these people back together" with a kiss, but to assess carefully the kinds of social pressures being exerted upon them by other people. This becomes the stuff of his separate conversations with them. He knows that it only adds fuel to the fire to talk to them together. But when he talks with them separately, the hidden "deals" that have been made with "the other woman" or "the other man" emerge. The threats that have been leveled by their mothers or fathers, brothers or sisters, of "never having anything to do with them again if they do go back to that brute or that wench" appear.

When we see couples in the quiet, silent desperation of the stage of private misunderstanding, we can involve them in group discussions along with those in the earlier stages of conflict. Sometimes group work will make it easier for them to open up to the leader on a personal basis. If a particularly loaded question comes at the pastor, he can ask if he can confer with the person for a moment after the group meeting so that he can give this more personal attention. At other times, the group work itself resolves the difficulty through straight inter-communion with other, more experienced couples. Reading helps some couples, but not nearly so many as we would think or like it to help. Simpler, briefer, nontechnical, and poetic material is of more use than the gobbledygook of much literature written by specialists in counseling. For example, one of the best self-help books on marriage was written by William Lyon Phelps, a professor of English literature! (*Marriage;* E. P. Dutton & Co., Inc., 1941.)

When we find couples in the years just prior to and following the birth of the first child, pastors should devise family-life discussion groups for them. This is the place to do preventive work, even more than with teen-agers. Here the couple find out that no marital choice is perfect, and that we learn to live with the one we *did* choose, not the one the books say we *should* have chosen.

The distinctly exhortative "use" of religion in this process is not as helpful as a consistent mood and atmosphere of prayer. The pastor has chosen to place his own personal faith between the lines of his conversations rather than in them. He loves God, not because he tries, but because God loved him and he can't help loving God now that he has encountered and been encountered by the Lord Jesus Christ. If this is so, and the pastor is not fooled in it, then the counselees have already felt it in the times together with the pastor. If it is not so, then all his special pleading about religion is in vain. Many counselees have heard this from their youth up, but an authentic person of faith in Christ is new every day to them. The first principles of the faith set forth in this book provide the basis for describing the very demonic itself at work in the shattering of marriages. The pastor's job requires that he be as wise as a serpent and as harmless as a dove in the confrontation of the distortions of sin. Such is the tension he bears as he participates in the ambiguity between the security the nuclear family offers and the freedom necessary for creative function that many sense is removed in the institution of marriage.

Indexes

AUTHOR INDEX

SUBJECT INDEX